# AUNT MARY

## MRS. PERRING

1st WORLD
LIBRARY
Literary Society

# Aunt Mary

## Mrs. Perring

© 1st World Library, 2007
PO Box 2211
Fairfield, IA 52556
www.1stworldlibrary.com
First Edition

LCCN: 2007930812

Softcover ISBN: 978-1-4218-4854-9
Hardcover ISBN: 978-1-4218-4757-3
eBook ISBN: 978-1-4218-4951-5

Purchase *"Aunt Mary"*
as a traditional bound book at:
www.1stWorldLibrary.com/purchase.asp?ISBN=978-1-4218-4854-9

1st World Library is a literary, educational organization
dedicated to:

- Creating a free internet library of downloadable ebooks

- Hosting writing competitions and offering book publishing
scholarships.

Interested in more 1st World Library books? contact:
literacy@1stworldlibrary.com
Check us out at: www.1stworldlibrary.com

# 1ˢᵗ World Library Literary Society

## Giving Back to the World

"If you want to work on the core problem, it's early school literacy."

**- James Barksdale, former CEO of Netscape**

"No skill is more crucial to the future of a child, or to a democratic and prosperous society, than literacy."

**- Los Angeles Times**

"Literacy... means far more than learning how to read and write... The aim is to transmit... knowledge and promote social participation."

**- UNESCO**

"Literacy is not a luxury, it is a right and a responsibility. If our world is to meet the challenges of the twenty-first century we must harness the energy and creativity of all our citizens."

**- President Bill Clinton**

"Parents should be encouraged to read to their children, and teachers should be equipped with all available techniques for teaching literacy, so the varying needs and capacities of individual kids can be taken into account."

**- Hugh Mackay**

# CHAPTER I

## AUNT MARY

In one of those very pretty suburban villas which are to be seen in the neighbourhood of all our large towns, Aunt Mary lived, at the time when my tale commences.

Indeed she had lived there the greater part of her life, for her father, Mr. Livesay, who had been a highly respected merchant in London for a great many years, had, unlike the generality of this prosperous class, retired from business as soon as he had secured a moderate competency for himself, his wife, and their four daughters, of whom our Aunt Mary was the eldest.

Mr. Livesay had purchased the pretty house, to which he had retreated from the hurry and bustle of the great city, but before doing so, he had taken care to ascertain that the inhabitants of the adjoining villa were likely to prove agreeable neighbours; and this he had done to his entire satisfaction, as Mr. and Mrs. Maitland, with their two sweet little children, gave promise of pleasurable society.

At the time of his retirement from business, the four daughters of Mr. Livesay were grown up to woman's estate; though perhaps that can hardly be said of the youngest,

Irene, who was only sixteen, while her two sisters, Ada and Alice, were of the respective ages of eighteen and twenty.

Great pains had been taken in the *real* education of these young ladies, for their excellent mother had spared no pains in their early training; and as they were all quick and clever children, the task of 'teaching the young idea how to shoot,' in their case, proved 'delightful.' We wish this were oftener the case; but to proceed: Aunt Mary, as we have said, was the eldest of these young ladies; she was at the discreet age of four-and-twenty—indeed, she might have been thirty, for the aptitude she displayed in household matters, taking all the care of housekeeping off her good mother's hands, and being looked up to, and appealed to, in all doubtful matters by her sisters.

Both Mr. and Mrs. Livesay considered their daughter Mary their chief treasure; indeed, she was everything that a daughter ought to be.

There was one thing, however, lacking that her three sisters possessed: she was not beautiful. Aunt Mary, if she had been pretty in infancy, had been spoiled by that dreadful ravager, the small-pox, which she had caught, through the carelessness of a nurse, when she was five years old.

It had not, however, left her entirely without good looks; for the kindly feelings of her heart beamed forth in the eloquent dark eyes and the sweet smile that almost invariably lighted up her face.

Laughingly, she used to say to her sisters, 'Well, you may all get married, and I shall live at home with my mother and father.'

And even as Aunt Mary said, so it came to pass: her sisters

Mrs. Perring

all married, and she remained at home, the loving daughter, the tender nurse, the deepest mourner for the loss of their dear parents, whom she had so dutifully cherished in their old age.

At the death of Mr. and Mrs. Livesay, which happened about ten years after the marriage of their two daughters, Ada and Alice—whom I must now introduce to the reader as Mrs. Ellis and Mrs. Beaumont—Aunt Mary was warmly entreated to give up housekeeping, and go and reside with one or other of her sisters, especially as Irene, the youngest, who had for the last twelve months undertaken the task of governess to the two Miss Maitlands, their next-door neighbours, was now engaged to be married, and the house, it was urged, would be too large and too lonely for Aunt Mary to reside in with any comfort.

This proposition, however, did not at all suit one who had for so many years acted independently; nor, although she was fond of children, would she on any account undertake a partial teaching of them. 'Let me have all the say, or none,' was Aunt Mary's maxim, so she decided to remain where she was, promising however, that when her sister Irene should marry Captain Gordon, she would take into serious consideration Mr. and Mrs. Maitland's earnest request, that she would continue the education of their two dear girls at her own house.

This, after the lapse of six months, Miss Livesay had agreed to, and had also sent for the eldest daughter of her sister Mrs. Beaumont, who was now a widow, with three children, though she had been left very well off, and could have sent her daughter Clara to a first-rate school, had she been so disposed. Mrs. Beaumont, however, knew too well the benefit her child was likely to derive from the real education she would receive from her sister Mary, to hesitate for a moment as to putting her under that lady's exclusive care; and thus at the same time that Oak Villa received Mrs. Maitland's two little girls, Annie and Dora, it became also the pleasant home of Clara Beaumont, who although she was the youngest of the trio, was certainly the most seriously disposed; perhaps, poor child, on account of the loss of her dear papa, who had died very unexpectedly, in the prime of life, from neglected cold, which terminated in acute bronchitis. This, though it had occurred six months previous to Clara's advent at Oak Villa, was an event still deeply felt and lamented by the sensitive child, and produced a seriousness of character seldom seen in children of her age; but the change was likely to prove very beneficial both to her health and spirits, and it was not long before Aunt Mary saw, with much pleasure, that her niece gladly entered upon her studies, and appeared very desirous to overtake her young companions in their several lessons, which, as she was exceedingly industrious, she was very likely to do before many weeks had passed away.

We must now, however, look after Aunt Mary's second sister, Mrs. Ellis, whose eldest daughter, Mabel, was only a few months older than Clara Beaumont, but whose character at this time was as unlike that of her young cousin as could possibly be imagined, which the reader will soon perceive when we introduce her in the next chapter, associated as she will be with the gentle and amiable daughters of Mrs. Maitland, who, together with her niece Clara, had been Aunt Mary's pupils for some months, though at present it was holiday-time.

# CHAPTER II

## A GREAT DISAPPOINTMENT

'Mamma dear,' said Dora Maitland, the eldest of that lady's two daughters, a sweet gentle-looking girl about twelve years of age, 'may Annie and I go and ask Mabel and Julia Ellis to take a walk with us this afternoon? We are going to see John Hutton's beehives; he has got some new glass ones, and he says it is so interesting to watch the little creatures at work. I am sure we should all like to see them, and I do so wish that Clara was here, to go with us, she is such a dear girl.'

While this request was making, Dora's younger sister, Annie, stood looking with beseeching eyes at mamma, evidently very anxious for that lady's reply, which was not immediately given, for Mrs. Maitland was apparently debating in her own mind whether it were desirable, or not, to attend to Dora's request.

'May we, mamma?' urged the young pleader timidly. 'You are not afraid to let us go, are you?' she inquired.

'Oh no, not afraid,' replied Mrs. Maitland; 'at least, not afraid of your going alone; but what I am afraid of is, that it may be inconvenient to Mrs. Ellis to let your young friends accompany you, as at present I know that their nurse is away, and—and she herself is not at all well.'

'Then do you think, mamma, that we may ask Julia to go with us? We like her best, and Mabel could stay at home and take care of the children, as she is the eldest.'

'Not a bad suggestion, my dear Dora,' replied her mother, 'only I fear there would be some objection on Mabel's part to such an arrangement. From what I have observed in that young lady,' continued Mrs. Maitland, 'she is not very loving, nor very tractable, and I fear she has been spoiled by over indulgence. However, if you will promise not to press the matter, should you see that it is likely to be inconvenient to Mrs. Ellis, you may go; it is a lovely afternoon, and I hope you will enjoy yourselves.'

With light hearts and buoyant footsteps, the two fair girls set off on their errand of inquiry to Camden Terrace, where Mr. Ellis resided, meeting with a very kind reception from Mrs. Ellis, and a joyful greeting from Mabel and Julia, who, to say the truth, were getting rather tired of the monotony of home, especially as, the nursemaid being away for a fortnight, and mamma not being well, they were under the necessity of taking care of the children, if care it could be called, where neither love nor forbearance were in exercise; but the little ones were only prevented from doing mischief, or hurting each other.

As the engagements of Mr. Ellis kept him from home all day, he had very little time, and I am sorry to say that he had very little inclination, to attend to his children, though we must do him the justice to say that he *wished* sincerely for their proper training; but he thought, as I fear too many papas do, that this duty belonged exclusively to his wife. This *we* think is a grave mistake. Children cannot be taught too early the lesson of obedience; and often it happens that the weakness or tenderness of a mother prevents her from enforcing this very salutary precept.

But I return to our young friends, who were under the necessity of making their request in the presence of both Mabel and Julia, though they had agreed between themselves not to do so, but to ask their mamma alone, so that if it were inconvenient to her they would not press the matter.

Without waiting for their mamma's answer, both the girls immediately begged to be allowed to go, indeed using every entreaty, so that poor Mrs. Ellis appeared quite distressed; and the young Maitlands were no less so, for they remembered what their mamma had said to them.

'I really scarcely know what to do,' said Mrs. Ellis, at last; 'I should be sorry to deprive you of any pleasure, but you know, Mabel, I am not well, and nurse is not with us: besides which, your papa made a particular request this morning that I would not let you go out to-day.'

'Oh, that is always the way with papa,' broke in Mabel, impetuously. 'I believe he would never let us go even for a walk, if he were at home.'

'Hush, hush, Mabel!' said her mother; 'I wonder you are not ashamed to speak of your papa in this disrespectful manner. Besides, you know that you are not speaking the truth.'

'Don't let them go, Mrs. Ellis, if it is inconvenient to you,' said Dora Maitland; 'we will call another day. I am sure mamma would be very sorry to hear that our coming brought any trouble to you.'

'It is not a trouble, of course,' again broke in the impetuous Mabel, without waiting her mamma's reply; 'and we shall be home long before papa, so nothing need be said to him about our having been out.'

The two young visitors looked at each other, and appeared quite distressed at this suggestion. They had been, and rightly so, taught to consider deception of any kind as falsehood; but Mrs. Ellis did not appear to be of the same opinion, and though she still urged her own ill health and the absence of the nurse, she was evidently inclined to yield to the continued and earnest request of her daughters.

'We will promise you not to be away more than an hour, dear mamma,' said Julia, who was certainly the best of the two girls; and this promise being seconded by Mabel very earnestly, poor Mrs. Ellis foolishly gave her consent to their going, which consent had no sooner been obtained, than the selfish girls darted off to make ready for their walk, leaving Dora and Annie very much concerned about what had passed, and determined in their own minds to forego the anticipated pleasure of seeing the glass beehives till a more convenient season, for fear they should not be back at the appointed time.

Mrs. Ellis, as I think I have before stated, had long been very delicate; she was of a nervous temperament, and nothing appeared to affect her health so much as excitement of any kind. She had been ordered lately to be kept perfectly quiet, but this is one of those rules that are more easily made than complied with by the mistress of a house, and the mother of a family; and, unfortunately for Mrs. Ellis, she had no strength of mind to aid her in the discharge of the duties that devolved upon her, for she was weakly indulgent both to her children, and her servants, and thus she was too often the slave of the one, and the dupe of the other.

After the young people had set off for their walk, she sat

down to consider whether she had done right in letting them go; and remembering her husband's prohibition, and the uncertainty of the time at which he would return home, she evidently came to an unfavourable conclusion in the matter, as she exclaimed aloud; 'I wish I had not let them go!'

Wishing, however, now, was of no avail, and as sundry screams from the nursery betokened a misfortune of some kind, the bell was rung for the cook to go, and ascertain the cause of the tumult. Fortunately, there was no great harm done: poor little Willie had contrived to mount on two boxes, which stood side by side, but not close enough together to prevent the chubby fat legs from slipping between them; and as Freddy and Gertrude in vain attempted to extricate the little fellow from his awkward position, they set up a simultaneous scream in token of their distress.

Kind-hearted Susan, however, soon set all to rights, for she was well-known to carry in her pocket sundry mysterious little sweet balls, which, if they were not over-clean, had a remarkable tendency to soothe, insomuch that sagacious Master Fred, seeing his sister Mabel one day crying with passion, inquired if he should go and ask Susan for one of her sugar balls, to do her good; a proposition which that young lady highly resented, though the very mention of the said sweets had stopped the crying.

But we must return to poor mamma, who had in vain endeavoured to follow Susan upstairs, she trembled so violently. When, however, Willie was placed on her knee, and she saw the slight nature of the hurt he had sustained, she began to feel more composed, for there was really no harm done.

The poor lady, however, was not suffered to calm down thus easily, for before Susan had time to quit the room, the sound of a key in the front door betokened the dreaded return of her husband, and again excited all her nervous fears.

'Why have you got the children with you, Ada?' said Mr. Ellis to his wife, reproachfully. 'You know that the doctor has told you to keep quiet.'

'Yes, I know,' replied Mrs. Ellis, meekly, 'but poor Willie has hurt his leg, so Susan brought him down to me.'

'But what has Susan to do with the children?' inquired Mr. Ellis. 'Surely Mabel and Julia are quite old enough to take care of them, without calling Susan from her work in the kitchen! Where are the girls?' demanded Mr. Ellis, sharply; 'I hope you have not let them go out after what I said this morning.'

'Mrs. Maitland's little girls came to ask them to take a walk, and I did not like to refuse them,' said Mrs. Ellis, timidly.

'Then I can only tell you, Ada,' said her husband, with suppressed passion, 'that by your foolish weakness you have deprived them of a great pleasure. It is not often that I can spare time to go out with them, but as I have had some tickets given me to go to a panorama, I have, at great inconvenience, come home, in order to take them, and you tell me that they are gone out.'

Poor Mrs. Ellis! This was a terrible mortification to her; she felt for her husband, and she felt for the disappointment of the girls, though they certainly deserved it.

'I am very sorry I let them go, dear Arthur,' she said, 'but they pressed me so much that I did not like to refuse.'

'Yes, yes,' said Mr. Ellis, 'I know; it is the old story: you are too weak-minded to refuse, and our children are to be ruined for want of proper restraint, or else *I* am to be appealed to in case of punishment, and so must be considered by them harsh and unkind. I cannot help saying that it is very cruel of you, Ada, to give way to this nervous weakness of yours,' continued Mr. Ellis, as he saw the poor lady begin to cry; 'the only way will be, I suppose, to send the girls to a boarding-school, before you have quite spoiled them.'

Having thus delivered his opinion, Mr. Ellis walked out of the room; and soon the rather violent shutting of the front door gave token that he had left the house, to the really great sorrow of his wife, who now heartily repented having given her consent to what had been the cause of so much trouble. But we must leave her to repent at leisure, and follow the gay young party, who, notwithstanding some few qualms of conscience on their first setting out, soon found plenty to interest them in the surrounding villas and gardens, where such diversity of taste is displayed.

## CHAPTER III

## THE LOST BROOCH

It was a lovely afternoon in the beginning of August. Some few fleecy clouds occasionally intercepted the rather too warm beams of the sun, from which our young friends intended to take shelter under the trees in the Regent's Park; for Dora and Annie Maitland had wisely determined not to mention Thomas Hutton and his glass beehives after what they had seen and heard at Camden Terrace, for they well knew that it would be impossible to walk that distance, and back again, in an hour.

'I have a beautiful book that my papa gave me yesterday,' said Dora Maitland; 'I thought you would like to see it, so I brought it with me. We can look at it while we sit to rest in the Park.'

'Oh yes, that will be delightful,' said Mabel; but she almost immediately added, 'I think I would rather look at the gay dresses of the ladies; we can look at books when we are at home.'

'Mabel is always talking about dress,' said her sister, laughing. 'I'm sure I don't care how I am dressed, if I am only clean and neat; it is such a trouble to be afraid of spoiling what one has on.'

Julia's opinion was echoed by Dora and Annie Maitland, so Mabel found she had no seconder; and they tripped along silently until they arrived at the desired spot for resting, a nice seat under the shade of a large tree. Here they were just going to seat themselves, when an exclamation from Mabel attracted the attention of the others, who inquired eagerly what was the matter.

'Oh, the brooch—mamma's beautiful brooch!' said the excited girl, in great distress; 'it is gone out of my necktie. Oh, what shall I do? what shall I do? It is mamma's favourite brooch; the one that papa gave her many years ago. Oh, I cannot go home without it!' continued Mabel, in a state of great distress.

'How could you be so foolish as to put it on, when you were only going for a country walk?' said Dora Maitland.

'I can't think why you should wear your mamma's brooch at all,' remarked Annie, 'unless she gave you leave.'

'But mamma did not give her leave; mamma has forbidden us to wear it,' said Julia, 'and I begged Mabel not to put it into her necktie to-day, for fear she should lose it; but she would do it, and now all our pleasure is spoilt.'

'You need not talk in that way,' angrily retorted her sister; 'you are fond enough of putting on mamma's gold chain when she leaves it out of the box, though she has often told you not to do so.'

'Hush, hush!' said Dora Maitland; 'quarrelling won't find the brooch; and see, there are a lady and gentleman coming toward us. Let us return home at once, the same way that we came: there were not many people on the road, and if we all look diligently we may find it, though I am much afraid that we shall not.'

This advice seemed the best that could be adopted by the young party, and they turned their steps homewards in no very enviable state of mind. There had been, indeed, much to damp the spirits, and prevent the enjoyment of this afternoon's walk. It is true that all around was beautiful, but that little monitor within, which insists upon being heard whether it is attended to or not, had acted like a thorn in the flesh to Mabel and Julia: and though Dora and Annie Maitland had nothing really to reproach themselves with, yet they could not forget the pale face of poor Mrs. Ellis, and her words of remonstrance to her selfish children seemed still to sound in their ears; and now they were returning home with a fresh trouble to the invalid lady.

Dora's beautiful book, which had been presented to her by her papa as a reward for her kind and dutiful attention to him, when he was suffering severely for some days from nervous headache, had of course not been thought of; the brooch, the unfortunate brooch, engrossed every faculty; yet with all the search, and research, it was not found, and the young people took a dolorous leave of each other, and repaired to their respective homes.

'Now don't you say a word about the brooch to mamma to-night,' said Mabel to her sister; 'I dare say it will be found, and it is no use teasing her about it, now she is poorly.

'Mamma is sure to miss the brooch off the dressing-table in the morning,' replied Julia; 'and if I am spoken to about it, I am not going to tell a story, Mabel.'

'Who wants you to tell a story?' exclaimed Mabel, sharply. 'I know you are always very ready to tell tales, when it would be much better for you to hold your tongue.'

'You always go on in that way when you are vexed about anything,' replied Julia. 'I'm sure I wish we had not gone for a walk; we have had no pleasure, all because you would try to make yourself look smart. You know, I begged of you not to put on the brooch, but, as papa says, you are so wilful!'

'You have no right to repeat what papa says. Better look at your own faults than talk about mine,' cried the angry girl, as she opened the garden-gate that led to the back door of their residence.

Freddy was looking out of the window, but Mabel took no notice of him, but ran straight upstairs to her own bedroom, to take off her things and examine minutely her dress, if happily the missing brooch might have slipped down into her bosom.

Julia, however, went to inquire how her mamma was, and therefore was the first to hear the dismal tidings that papa had come home on purpose to take his daughters to a place of entertainment, but finding they were not at home, had gone out again very angry, without eating any dinner. This, though it put the finishing stroke to that day's disaster, poor Julia knew would not be an end to the troubles they would have to encounter; for though indeed she was innocent of blame with regard to the brooch, she felt she had acted selfishly in leaving her mamma with the children, when she saw how tired and poorly Mrs. Ellis appeared to be.

'I am very sorry, dear mamma,' said Julia, 'that you have been so troubled with the children; I hoped that Susan would have minded them while we were out.'

'Well, go now and take off your things, my dear,' replied Mrs. Ellis; 'then you and Mabel can have tea in the nursery with the children, while I rest on the sofa.'

'Yes, dear mamma; they shall go with me at once,' said Julia. 'Come, Freddy; come, Gerty; and come, little Willie,' she added, as she took the chubby hand in her own, and was leading him away, when her mamma said, 'Mind you don't hurt his poor leg, Julia, for he has fallen and scraped the skin off.'

'Oh, poor boy!' said his sister, as she took Willie up in her arms; 'let us go and put a "passer" on it.' This was always what the little fellow called out for, when he hurt himself: 'Oh, put a "passer" on—put a "passer" on!'

Mabel was very glad when Julia brought up the children, and told her that their mamma was lying down on the sofa, for she had no wish to talk just then with anybody. She felt indeed much disquieted, but what her feelings were when her sister related the circumstance of their papa's coming home, on purpose to take them to a place of amusement, may be more easily imagined then described; and yet we fear that self-reproach did not, in the smallest degree, mingle with their feelings, so little do some people know of *self*.

# CHAPTER IV

## THE RECOVERED TREASURE

It was with a feeling of great uneasiness that Mabel awoke the next morning. She had not at all made up her mind what to do. She was, as I have shown, a very selfish girl, and not by any means of a good disposition; indeed, I should say, that no selfish person could be. But she was not in the habit of telling direct falsehoods, though she did not scruple to prevaricate, if such a course suited her purpose; and this practice is certainly not only near akin to falsehood, but leads directly to it.

Nothing was said at breakfast-time to make any disturbance, and papa went out as usual; while Mabel and Julia, with minds still oppressed by the loss on the preceding day, requested mamma to permit them to take the children for a walk, before they began lessons.

'It is such a lovely morning,' said Mabel, 'and we can go towards the Park, the same way that we went yesterday.'

Of course the brooch was uppermost in Mabel's mind, and indeed in Julia's too, though nothing was then said.

'I  am quite willing that you should all go, my dears,' said the kind mother; 'only remember, little Willie can't walk as fast and as far as you can.'

'Et me tan, ma; me walk a long, long way wid pa, and me not tired a bit,' said Willie, shaking his curly poll, and running off with Julia, who was his favourite, to get dressed.

'Susan, where's my gold brooch?' inquired Mrs. Ellis of the servant, who happened to be in the bedroom dusting, when her mistress entered.

'I don't know, I'm sure, ma'am,' replied Susan. 'I saw it on the pincushion yesterday, before the young ladies went out; I have not seen it since. Perhaps Miss Mabel may be wearing it.'

'Nonsense, Susan!' said Mrs. Ellis; 'how could you think Miss Mabel would do such a thing without my leave?'

'Well, ma'am,' answered the steady servant, 'I don't know whether you gave leave or not, but I know I have often seen the young lady with the brooch in her necktie.'

Mrs. Ellis felt greatly displeased, not of course with Susan, but with her daughter; she thought it best, however, to make no further remark at present, but to wait until Mabel returned for an explanation of the affair.

It is almost needless to say that the morning's walk had neither been pleasant nor satisfactory to the two girls, for the treasure they went out to seek had not been found, and they returned home sick at heart. I say 'they,' because though poor Julia had not been really to blame, she sorrowed both on her mamma's and her sister's account; besides which, she had a dread of her papa's coming to the knowledge of the untoward event.

'Mabel,' said Mrs. Ellis, as soon as that young lady came in, 'have you had my brooch on to-day?'

'No, mamma,' was the immediate and the only response to the question, the words *to-day* forming a loophole to creep out at, so as to avoid explanation, though that was the very time to make one. Accordingly search was again commenced —as we know, without any result.

The midday dinner-hour passed away uncomfortably enough, except for the little folks, whose appetite did not seem to be in the least impaired by surrounding circums-tances; and strange as it may appear, Mrs. Ellis, notwith-standing what the servant had told her respecting Mabel's wearing the brooch, instead of closely questioning that young lady, permitted her to leave the room with the children, while she herself renewed the fruitless search. Tired out at last, she sat down in the dining-room, to await the coming home of her husband in no very pleasurable state of mind. Of course she must tell him of her loss; but she well knew how angry he would be, and what a commotion was likely to ensue. However, there was no help for it.

'Ada,' said Mr. Ellis to his wife, after he had enjoyed a comfortable dinner, and had taken his customary seat in the arm-chair, newspaper in hand, 'what has become of that valuable brooch that I gave you on your birthday? You used to wear it every day; why have you not got it on now?'

The usually pale face of Mrs. Ellis flushed all over at this inquiry, but she answered truthfully—Mabel had certainly not learned to tell falsehoods, either from her mamma or papa:

'I am very sorry to tell you, Arthur,' said Mrs. Ellis, 'that the brooch is missing; I have searched in vain for it, and Susan does not know anything about it.'

'Have you inquired of the girls, and the children?' said Mr. Ellis; 'perhaps they may have seen it.'

'I did ask Mabel when she came in from her walk if she had had it on,' replied the lady,' and she said she had not.'

'Call Mabel and Julia down, and let me question them,' said papa; 'perhaps I may learn more about the brooch than you think.'

'Oh, I'm sure it is no use, my dear,' replied Mrs. Ellis, dreading a scene, for she knew how severely her husband was inclined to visit faults which she, poor lady, had not courage to grapple with. 'Better not disturb yourself about the brooch to-night,' she added; 'we will have another search for it to-morrow, and I am sure the girls know nothing about it.'

'*I* am not sure of any such thing,' replied Mr. Ellis, 'and I insist upon Mabel and Julia being told to come to me.'

As there was no resisting her husband's authority, the girls were summoned to their papa's presence; and though they knew not why it was, there was a conscious uneasiness in their minds which certainly did not lend wings to their feet.

'Come here, girls,' said their papa, though not in an unkindly tone, as they entered the dining-room. 'I want to ask you a few questions. Mind, I must have truthful and straight-forward answers—no prevarication.'

Mrs. Ellis looked at the two girls, and then at her husband, with astonishment, not having the least idea of what was coming; yet she felt very uneasy.

Mrs. Perring

'Mabel,' said Mr. Ellis, addressing his eldest daughter, 'you were out yesterday?'

'Yes, papa,' replied that young lady; 'Julia and I went for a walk with Dora and Annie Maitland.'

'And where did you go?' was the next inquiry, and one very easily answered.

'To the Regent's Park, papa,' said Julia; 'but we were there only a short time.'

'Now just one more question, and I have done,' said papa; 'did either of you girls lose anything while you were out?'

'Oh, papa, yes,' answered Julia instantly—'mamma's brooch. Oh, have you found it, papa?' she exclaimed.

'Mamma's brooch!' said Mr. Ellis, with a look of assumed astonishment. 'Why, which of you presumed to wear your mamma's brooch?' But he added almost immediately, 'I need not inquire further: I am sorry to say I have had some sad experience of deception in my eldest daughter, and have observed in her that silly vanity, that makes outside show a cover for inward defects. Go!' he added sternly to Mabel; 'I have nothing more to say to you to-night. It nearly sickens me to think that I have a daughter base enough to conceal faults, which she is not afraid of committing.'

With conscious shame and distress, Mabel quitted the dining-room; and Julia also was retreating, when her papa told her to remain, as he had something to say to her.

Though Julia felt very sorry for her sister, and would have been glad to speak a word of comfort to her, yet she was so anxious to hear from her papa something about the lost brooch, that she was not at all reluctant to remain; so planting herself by her mother's side, she stood patiently to listen to what further Mr. Ellis had to say.

'Did you know, Julia, that Mabel had on your mamma's brooch when you went for a walk?' inquired papa.

Julia hung down her head, yet she answered truthfully;

'Yes, papa, I did know, for I begged her not to wear it.'

'And when she persisted in doing so, why did you not appeal to your mamma?'

To this question there came no response, so Mr. Ellis continued:

'Let me warn you, my little girl,' he said kindly, 'never to connive at faults in your brothers or sisters; it is to them a cruel kindness, which both they and you may live to be sorry for in after life.'

As Mr. Ellis said this, he drew from his waistcoat-pocket the glittering trinket, which had been the innocent cause of so much anxiety, and placing it in his wife's hand, said:

'Now, my dear, I advise you to be more careful of your *jewels*, or you may lose far more precious ones than this brooch.'

As he made this remark he nodded to Julia, though Mrs. Ellis well understood what her husband meant.

'Now, my little girl, you may go and join the children, while I tell mamma how I came by the brooch.'

# CHAPTER V

## A FRIEND IN NEED

Julia was very glad indeed to see the brooch again, and glad also to receive a dismissal, as she longed to tell her sister the good news.

'And now, my dear,' said Mr. Ellis, when they were alone, 'I suppose you want to learn the particulars respecting the lost and found.'

'Indeed I do, Arthur,' replied his wife; 'it seems a marvellous thing to me how the brooch should have come into your possession, or indeed how it was found at all.'

'Well, it all came about without any magic, as you shall hear,' said her husband. 'You remember the young lady, Miss Vernon, who was staying a short time in the winter with our friends the Maitlands, and whom we were invited to meet?'

'Oh yes, I remember her quite well; I thought her so very pretty, and she sang so delightfully. But what of her?' inquired Mrs. Ellis.

'Well,' replied the gentleman, 'that lady is now a Mrs. Norton; she is married to a friend of mine—an old friend, I should say, for we went to school together.'

'Then he must be considerably older than the lady,' said Mrs. Ellis, 'for I think she is not twenty yet.'

'You are right there, my dear,' said her husband; 'I dare say Norton is twice her age: but he is a fine-looking man—and,' added Mr. Ellis, with a significant smile, 'he has plenty of money, Ada: you know what a bait that is for the ladies.'

'No, I don't know any such thing, Arthur,' replied the lady, warmly; 'and I don't like to hear such things said. Men much oftener marry for money than women do.'

'Well, we will discuss that point some other time, my dear,' said Mr. Ellis; 'but now for my story:

'As I was walking through the Strand this morning, who should I meet but the couple we were speaking of. I did not know them at first, but as they stopped short, and prevented my passing, I soon recognised both lady and gentleman, though it is many years since I saw the latter.

'After the usual congratulations and shaking of hands had been gone through, my friend said:

'"Well, I certainly did not expect to meet you here, Ellis, though, strange to say, you are the very person we came out to call upon; for, strangely enough, I have in my possession a brooch, which, I feel sure, must belong to your good wife, as it has her name, Ada Ellis, engraven on the back. Am I right?" added Norton, taking the brooch from his pocket, and handing it to me.

'"Yes," I said, "this is certainly my wife's brooch, but how it could come into your possession is a mystery to me."

"It need not be so long, if you will just walk into the Temple Gardens with us. I am going to call on a friend there, and we shall be out of all this noise and bustle," said Norton.

'As I was not just then under any engagement, I turned back with them, and heard the story of the lost and found. It is a very simple one, and I give it in his own words,' said Mr. Ellis.

"'You know Mr. and Mrs. Maitland," began Mr. Norton; "my wife says that she met you at their house last winter, and as they are very old and kind friends of hers, and our stay in town will be short, we set off yesterday morning to call upon them. Unfortunately, the two nice little girls were out, so we did not see them, though I hope we shall do so before we leave London. After leaving Mr. Maitland's, we strolled towards the Regent's Park; and when we had pretty well tired ourselves, we made towards a pleasant seat under the shade of a magnificent tree. A party of young ladies were just leaving the spot which we had selected, but as they were intently looking on the ground, with their backs towards us, they, I suppose, did not notice our approach; nor could we, at the distance we were, recognise them.

"'In this pleasant spot we remained for some time, and on rising to go, my wife saw just at her foot, though it was partially hidden by a tuft of grass, the valuable brooch which I have just had the pleasure to restore to you, and which it was our intention to place in your hands at your own home, had we not thus accidentally met you. Very glad indeed I am that we should have come upon the track of the young ladies, who could be none other but the little Maitlands and your fair daughters. To-morrow, I hope to bring my wife to Camden Terrace, and to introduce her to your good lady as Mrs. Norton, instead of Laura Vernon."

'Now, my dear,' said Mr. Ellis, 'you have got your brooch, and its recent history. I strongly advise you to take more care of the one, and on no account to forget the other.'

'I will try to take your advice, my dear,' said the lady. 'I am so glad, so very glad, that my brooch is found.'

'And I am so sorry, so very sorry, Ada,' said Mr. Ellis, 'that we have a daughter so prone to the detestable vices of pride, vanity, and deceit!'

'Oh, don't be too hard upon poor Mabel, dear,' said her mamma; 'she is very young. You must forgive this childish trick.'

'Trick!' said Mr. Ellis, bitterly—'yes, you have given it a right name, Ada; but I hate tricks.'

# CHAPTER VI

## A FRIENDLY PROPOSITION

The morning after the foregoing occurrence found Mabel very dull, and very captious. She was of course glad to know that the brooch had been found, but very uneasy at the manner of finding it. She was not, in truth, sorry for the fault that she had committed, but her proud spirit chafed at the idea of being talked about in the Maitland family, especially as she knew that a young cousin of theirs, Harry Maitland, was expected to pay them a visit on this very day, when the whole affair was sure to be canvassed.

But we will leave Mabel to her own uneasy thoughts, and look in at the pleasant family party assembled in the break-fast-room of the Laurels, as Mr. Maitland's residence was designated. This villa, as we know, adjoined that of Aunt Mary, who at this time was on a visit with her niece Clara to that young lady's widowed mother, Mrs. Beaumont. Cousin Harry had arrived, and made one of the happy group, who were sitting, books and work in hand, for they were never idle, enjoying the fresh pure air of the morning, and the delicious smell of flowers, of which there was a profusion both outside and in. The garden, indeed, was resplendent with variety and beauty of colouring, softly shaded down by the laurels, which gave their name to the villa.

Mr. Maitland had been reading a book of travels, and he was now descanting on the uses and properties of the Eucalyptus, or blue gum-tree of Australia, which is said to grow as much in seven years, as an oak will grow in twenty; attains sometimes the height of three and four hundred feet, drains the ground, attracts rain, prevents malaria, etc.

'But do you really believe, sir, all that is written about this wonderful tree?' inquired Harry Maitland, who had been making a sketch of the said tree, from the description which his uncle had been reading to them.

'Certainly, I do believe all that is stated of it,' replied Mr. Maitland. 'Why should I doubt well-accredited writers and eye-witnesses? The most extraordinary fact respecting it is, its health-diffusing properties, which, as I read, makes me wonder why strenuous efforts have not been made for its cultivation in England. I know there have been, and there are, some efforts made, but not on an extensive scale. There are some young trees in the Kew Gardens, which, before you leave us, Harry, I hope we shall go to see.'

Just as Mr. Maitland was beginning to read again, he was interrupted by a smart rap-tap at the front door; and immediately after, the servant announced Mr. and Mrs. Norton.

'Dear Laura,' exclaimed Mrs. Maitland, kissing her young friend,' I am very glad to see you again, though I did not expect you would be out so early this morning. I see,' added the lady, 'I need not introduce Dora and Annie; though you did not see them yesterday, it is evident they have not forgotten you.'

Indeed they had not, for each had seized a hand of their favourite, and had given and received a warm salute.

While these kindly salutations were going on, Mr. Maitland and Harry were exchanging courtesies with their friend Mr. Norton, for Cousin Harry was no stranger to that gentleman, who had often been a visitor at his father's house—or rather I should say rectory, in Kent—always an agreeable one, for he had travelled much, and could make himself a most interesting companion.

'I did not tell you yesterday, Mr. Maitland,' said their visitor, 'that we leave England for Australia in a week's time; I know under the circumstances you will excuse this early and unceremonious visit, as we wish to spend as much time as possible with our friends, and to have some little excursions with the young people.'

'Are you really going to leave England so soon, and going so far away?' inquired Mr. Maitland, rather dolefully. 'I am so sorry for our own sakes, but I hope it will be to your own great advantage.'

'Yes, I hope so too,' replied Mr. Norton; 'our prospects are very fair; the climate is good, and I have many friends located there.'

'And you will be in the native land of this magnificent tree we have been reading about,' said Harry, 'the blue gum tree. Do, Mr. Norton, write and tell us all you know about it.'

'Harry is quite sceptical respecting its merits,' said Mr. Maitland, laughing. 'I do hope you will be able to convince him that what he has read and heard about it is all quite true.'

'I am sorry to say that I have never yet turned my attention to the subject, but I make Master Harry a promise that I will do so, and that I will give him all possible information I can gain on the subject; but just now,' added the gentleman, 'we have a proposal to make, which we must not defer, as our time is so short. It is this,' continued Mr. Norton, 'that we all spend a pleasant day together at some place of amusement, to be chosen by the young ladies. We are to spend this evening at Camden Terrace, with our kind friends Mr. and Mrs. Ellis. I hope you will be there, and then we can settle our plans for to-morrow.'

'We have been invited,' said Mrs. Maitland, 'but unfortunately we had a prior engagement; but I promise you, Mr. Norton, that in whatever direction you may decide to go to-morrow, we will accompany you.'

'Stop, stop, my dear,' interrupted Mr. Maitland; 'you are reckoning without your host, although he happens to be in the room with you. Do you forget that I have to set off early in the morning to pay a visit to a sick friend who is particularly anxious to see me?'

'Well, we shall be very sorry to go without you, Maitland,' replied Mr. Norton; 'but I suppose Master Harry, here, will try to supply your place to the young ladies, and we must do as well as we can.'

'Did you hear about our finding Mrs. Ellis's brooch yesterday, in the Regent's Park?' inquired Mrs. Norton; 'but perhaps you have not seen any of them. It was a curious accident.'

'The brooch!' exclaimed Dora and Annie, simultaneously. 'Did you really find the brooch? Oh, we are so glad! We told dear mamma about it, and she was as sorry as we were, but we have not seen Mabel or Julia since. How did you happen to find it, Mrs. Norton?'

'We went to seat ourselves under the shade of the trees,'

Mrs. Perring

replied the lady. 'We saw you in the distance, but did not know who you were; and I dare say you did not see us, for you were all looking on the ground.'

'Yes, of course we were,' said Dora; 'we were searching for the brooch. And I remember we did see a lady and gentleman coming towards us; we went away sooner on that account, for Mabel was in such a temper I felt ashamed of anyone coming near us, though she was the only person to blame, as she ought not to have worn her mamma's brooch.'

'Hush, hush! my little girl!' said papa; 'don't you know that our motto is, "If you cannot speak good of a person, say nothing at all of them."'

'Bravo! bravo!' cried Mr. Norton. 'I heartily wish that this golden rule were adopted in every family. What a world of trouble would be saved, and how much more time there would be for profitable conversation!'

'Well,' said Mrs. Maitland, 'we are all heartily glad that the treasure is recovered; and perhaps its temporary loss, and the uneasiness it occasioned, may be a useful lesson to the young people.'

The visitors now took leave of their friends, promising themselves the pleasure of seeing them in the morning, at the early hour of eleven, in order that they might have a long day together. It was also agreed that, to save time and trouble, the parties were to meet at the Park, if no objection were raised to the proposed plan by Mr. and Mrs. Ellis.

# CHAPTER VII

## THE ZOOLOGICAL GARDENS

It was a lovely day, this 10th of August; there was scarcely a cloud to be seen in the sky. The trees, it is true, were beginning to put on their russet tints here and there, but this only added to the beauty of their colouring; there certainly was at present no disagreeable appearance of coming changes.

It had been agreed, on the preceding evening, that Mr. and Mrs. Norton should call for Mabel and Julia, as Mr. Ellis had declared that he could not spare time for a day's pleasure, and poor Mrs. Ellis said that she felt too weak at present to undertake the task of wandering about in the Gardens.

This was a great disappointment to their friends the Nortons, who were not quite sure that Mrs. Maitland would be able to accompany her young people, as she had intimated a doubt on the subject before they bade adieu on the preceding evening: however, they made up their minds that it would be a pleasant day for the juveniles. Mr. Ellis had strongly objected to Mabel's making one of the party; he insisted that it would be only a proper punishment to deprive her of the pleasure on account of the recent delinquency. He was, however, over-ruled in his opinion, both by his wife and his friends, and so, very reluctantly, he was induced to give up the point.

As usual, Mabel's first consideration in the morning, after her papa had gone out, was what she should wear on this eventful day; and on her mamma's suggesting that she and Julia should put on their grey dresses, she was vehemently opposed by that young lady, who declared she would rather stay at home than go to the Gardens with Mr. and Mrs. Norton in such a dowdy dress.

Julia, on the contrary, was quite content to follow her mamma's advice, as she very wisely agreed that if they put on their light silk dresses, they might have them soiled, or perhaps spoiled. This idea, however, was treated with contempt by Mabel, and the young lady waxed so warm in the discussion, that the too indulgent, peace-loving Mrs. Ellis gave way, and gave permission to her daughters to do as they thought proper, only she warned them that they had no time to lose.

Away tripped the sisters to make ready—Julia with a determination to follow her mamma's advice, Mabel with the intention of keeping her own foolish resolve of pride and vanity.

An obstacle, however, presented itself on the first putting on of the silk dress: it had not been worn for some time, as during the summer muslins had superseded silk, and Mabel found, to her great disgust, that the sleeves were too short. She had certainly known of this before, but as she was by no means remarkable for provident care of her clothes, in taking pains to keep them in order, a button wanting, or a rent unmended, or a sleeve too short, were things not at all to be wondered at in Mabel's wardrobe.

'How provoking!' she exclaimed, as she looked at her wrists; 'I cannot possibly go out unless I have under-sleeves, and I haven't a pair.'

'Oh, do as mamma wished,' said Julia; 'put on your grey frock. You will be much more comfortable, because you won't be afraid of spoiling it.'

'Hold your tongue, you foolish little thing,' replied Mabel. 'I tell you I wouldn't be seen out with Mr. and Mrs. Norton, with such a dress as you are wearing; besides,' she continued, 'Harry Maitland will be with his cousins.'

'And what of that?' exclaimed Julia, in astonishment; 'surely you don't mind what he thinks about your dress!'

There was no direct answer to this remark, but Mabel declared she was not going to submit to her younger sister's dictation; and as a capital idea seemed just then to strike her, she went to one of the small drawers which indeed belonged to her mamma, and took from thence a pair of beautiful lace sleeves and proceeded to put them on.

'Oh, don't, don't!' cried Julia; 'pray do not wear those beautiful sleeves of mamma's! you know dear Aunt Mary gave them to her, and as they are her work, mamma values them so much! Pray remember the brooch,' she added; 'or if you will persist in putting them on, go and ask leave first.'

'I mean to ask mamma when we go downstairs,' said Mabel, 'but you know I have not time now. I wish you would not be so officious with your advice and your cautions, just as if I didn't know how to act as well as you do.'

With the promise that mamma should be spoken to, Julia was obliged to be satisfied, as a loud tapping at the front-door betokened the arrival of their friends Mr. and Mrs. Norton; and the two girls hastily finished their dressing and their discussion, and went down to join their friends.

Whether, in the hurry of salutations and leave-taking, Mabel actually *forgot* her promise to speak to her mamma about the sleeves, we shall not undertake to say; certain it is, that there was no mention made of them. And the party set off in high spirits to join their young friends the Maitlands, as had been agreed, at the gate of the Zoological Gardens.

There had been strict punctuality on both sides, for neither party had to wait.

But great was Mabel's mortification to find Dora and Annie had, like her sister Julia, dressed themselves in their plain grey frocks, so *she* looked like a golden pheasant among a set of barn-door fowls: and however much vanity she possessed, her common sense taught her that she had laid herself open to ridicule; though of course no one spoke of her dress, and even the beautiful sleeves seemed at the time to attract no attention.

In a very short time, the whole party were intently gazing with wonder and admiration on the marvels of creation.

The elephants, the giraffe, the rhinoceros, the hippopotamus, etc., all passed in review, and elicited remarks of wonder and astonishment from the young visitors, such as their monstrous size and great strength were well calculated to draw forth. The lions, tigers, leopards and bears came in for a share of applause; but as the strength of these animals is not evidenced by their size, I must acknowledge they were taken less notice of than either the huge creatures or the smaller and more elegant and delicate quadrupeds, which, generally speaking, won the admiration of the party. The bipeds, we may be sure, were not neglected; but the congregated tribe of them kept up such an incessant clatter, that having borne it for some little time, Harry Maitland was fain to stop his ears and run out of their house, declaring that 'their noise was worse than could be made by a hundred scolding women.' A very ungallant declaration, certainly, for a young gentleman, and one that he had not, and was never likely to have, the opportunity of proving the truth of. Harry was soon joined by the young ladies, whom the noise of the parrot-house had nearly deafened, and a general resolution was put, and carried by the whole party, Mabel herself not excepted, that fine plumage did not at all make amends for disagreeable propensities.

'And now,' said Harry Maitland, with just one sly glance at the bright silk frock, whose wearer was standing beside him, 'suppose we go and pay a visit to our friends the monkeys? That is to say, young ladies,' he added, 'if you don't think it would be jumping out of the frying-pan into the fire, and can endure smell better than noise.'

'Oh yes!' was the general exclamation; 'do let us go and see the monkeys.'

'Who has got any biscuits or nuts?' inquired Dora Maitland. 'I haven't got anything.'

'I have some pieces of biscuit left from what I bought for the elephants,' said Mabel.

'And I have nuts in my pocket,' said Harry; 'while the monkeys are cracking them, we can be cracking our jokes.' But these proved to be rather unpleasant ones, to one at least of the party, who, nevertheless, as she could not foresee what was coming, was the first to laugh at Harry's silly speech.

The monkey-house proved, as they thought it would, anything but agreeable to the olfactory nerves of our young friends; though their attention was soon diverted from what was offensive, by the very amusing gymnastics of the monkeys, who, while they performed their various feats of skill, had evidently an eye to the main chance, and kept a vigilant look-out for something more substantial than applause.

'Give this old fellow a bit of your biscuit, Mabel,' said Dora Maitland; 'he is evidently expecting some from us.'

Now we know that monkeys, though they are anxious expectants, are not very gracious receivers, which poor Mabel, who seemed to, be the doomed person, found to her cost, when, on stretching out her arm to give the required morsel, the ungrateful recipient caught hold of the beautiful lace sleeve, tore it from her arm, doubled it up in an instant, and thrust it into his mouth, clambering with great rapidity to the very top of his habitation, as if afraid of pursuit, and looking down with a hideous grin on the astonished and disgusted parties below.

'Oh, poor mamma's beautiful lace sleeve!' ejaculated Julia, to the great annoyance of the trembling and affrighted Mabel, on whom all eyes were now turned.

'Oh, what a pity! what a pity!' sounded on every side; but there was no redress, and Mabel, unable to restrain her tears, or to give vent to her varied feelings of anger, scorn, and vexation, rushed out of the monkey-house, leaving Julia to explain, and her friends to condole. All the party except Harry Maitland had before seen, and very greatly admired, these sleeves of Mrs. Ellis's, which, as I said before, were Aunt Mary's work; and sorry, very sorry, were both Dora and Annie Maitland to hear that Mabel had put them on without her mamma's leave. 'Well, it's no use being sorry now,' cried Harry Maitland; 'we can't restore the sleeve, that's certain. I wonder how girls can be so foolish as to dress themselves up, when they come to such a place as this—especially,' he added sarcastically, 'in other people's finery.'

'I am glad Mabel was not near enough to hear your remarks, Harry,' said his cousin Dora; 'I am sure she must be quite enough troubled, without our saying anything disagreeable.'

'Yes, but she brought the trouble upon herself, and therefore she deserves to suffer,' persisted Harry; 'the worst of it is,' he added, 'she makes innocent people suffer for her fault.'

'Let us go and see after Mabel,' said the kind-hearted Annie; 'I think we have all had enough of the monkeys to-day.'

'Yes, one young lady has had rather too much of them,' said Harry, 'or rather, I should say, the monkey has had too much of her; though the old fellow appears to be quite satisfied with the trick he has played.'

'There is Mabel,' cried Julia, as they came out of the monkey-house. 'Poor thing, don't let us say anything more about the sleeve; I am sure she must feel very uncomfortable.'

'I wonder where we shall find Mr. and Mrs. Norton,' said Dora; 'we have been a long time away from them: perhaps they are looking after us.'

'I'll tell you where I think they are,' said Harry; 'it is about the time for the sea-lion to exhibit himself, and we had better bend our steps that way, for we are almost sure of finding the lady and gentleman there;' and it proved to be the fact, for among the numerous spectators which the sea-lions had attracted, our young friends soon singled out Mr. and Mrs. Norton. The flushed face and tear-swollen eyes of Mabel did not escape the notice of the lady, but seeing that she turned away, and appeared anxious to avoid observation, Mrs. Norton made no remark, and soon all the party were interested spectators of the various exploits of the marine prodigy.

Suddenly, however, a violent plunge of the animal into the water, on the side near which our friends were standing, sent a rather unpleasant shower-bath among the crowd, and caused a sudden retreat, though it did not take place in time for all of them to avoid a wetting. I am sorry to say that Mabel's silk frock came in for a share; but this would not really have mattered much, if, in her hurry to get out of the way, she had not unfortunately set her foot on the skirt of it, which made her fall on one knee, and thus come in contact with the wet soil and gravel, which, however harmless they might have proved to a grey dress, by no means improved the colour of a light silk one. 'Misfortunes never come alone,' it is said; and though I am not myself a firm believer in this proverb, it certainly proved true with regard to Mabel Ellis, though these misfortunes were entirely the results of her pride and self-will, so she does not deserve our commiseration.

It was evident, too, that she did not wish for sympathy just then, for brushing off the soil from her dress, and making very light of the matter, she seemed to say: 'I don't want your sympathy; please to keep it to yourselves.'

Of course my readers will not suppose that the young lady really was indifferent to the spoiling of her dress, but she had so much silly pride in her composition, that she thought to appear sorry would lower her in the eyes of her companions. She certainly did not judge *them* correctly, nor had she as yet, poor girl, reached the climax of her troubles; but for this we must go a little further, and see the party comfortably seated at one of the marble tables in the elegant refreshment-rooms, where tea, and sandwiches, and buns are plentifully provided, and highly appreciated by the young ramblers after their long walk and sight-seeing, which are both very exhausting, and require refreshment, and relaxation, and rest. Seated round this pleasant table, and in the enjoyment of the good things that were placed thereon, the spirits of the young ones of the party rose considerably; and Harry Maitland, who was quick-witted and fond of joking, created plenty of juvenile mirth by his remarks upon the monkey tribe, though of course he avoided saying anything that might lead to unpleasant inquiries.

It happened, unfortunately, that when the lace sleeve had been so ruthlessly torn from Mabel's arm by the audacious monkey, it did not occur to that young lady to make sure of the other sleeve by taking it off and putting it into her pocket. Instead of acting thus prudently, she contented herself with tucking the lace up under its elastic band—a very treacherous safeguard, as it proved.

Our friend Harry, as the young squire of the party, was very attentive to the ladies, as indeed he always was; but it happened unfortunately that in handing a plate of buns to his opposite neighbour, Mabel, he became the innocent cause of another disaster to that most luckless damsel, for the lace that had been so unceremoniously tucked out of sight, having escaped from the elastic band, attached itself to the handle of Mabel's cup, as she reached out her hand to take the offered bun, and upset the whole of its contents, which, though the greater part of the fluid went into the saucer, quite sufficient found its way into Mabel's dress to put the finishing stroke to her misfortunes.

Hastily jumping up, and without waiting for any condolence or assistance, the excited girl rushed out of the room, followed by Julia, whose kind heart really ached to see her sister so distressed.

'Don't follow them out, my dears,' said Mrs. Norton to Dora and Annie Maitland, who had risen from their chairs to do so. 'I am sure,' she continued, 'that Mabel would much rather be without your sympathy, and you cannot possibly render her any assistance. Poor foolish girl,' added the lady, 'I cannot say I am sorry for *her*; but I well know what trouble she must give her mamma, whom I really am sorry for.'

'But, Laura dear,' inquired Mr. Norton, 'don't you suspect that some blame must attach itself to the young lady's mother? Faults, you know, like ill weeds, grow apace if they are not corrected; and the weeds, if suffered to grow rank, will destroy the beautiful flowers which we expected to see in our gardens. Is it not so, do you think?'

'Yes, you are quite right, no doubt,' replied the lady; 'and I fear that my poor friend, Mrs. Ellis, will find it very difficult, if not impossible, to correct faults, which, through weak indulgence, seem to have taken deep root. But,' added Mrs. Norton, rising to go, 'this is no place for sermonising. We have had a pleasant day, notwithstanding the troubles of our young friends; we had better look after them now, and wend our way homewards.'

# CHAPTER VIII

## A BITTER DISAPPOINTMENT

'No, my dear, I am determined that Mabel shall not go with her sister to Mrs. Maitland's juvenile party. You over-ruled my wish yesterday, and suffered her to go to the Gardens, and I think you have been properly punished for that' (alluding to the sleeves). 'To-day I insist on having my way. It is most painful to me to see, as I cannot help doing, that through your weakness of character, or want of discipline, Mabel has grown up to be a plague to us, instead of a comfort.'

This unwelcome truth was uttered by Mr. Ellis before he left home on the morning after the visit to the Gardens; and he added, before he left the room:

'I am very glad that your sister, Aunt Mary, is coming home this week, for I intend to ask her as a particular favour to take Mabel under her care. I wish we had sent her to Oak Villa twelve months ago; we might have been spared much trouble.'

This parting rebuke and warning had the usual effect of making Mrs. Ellis very nervous; she could not bear the thought of communicating the ill news it contained to Mabel.

She had come to have almost a childish dread of the girl's temper, yet she knew well that her husband's mandate must be obeyed. There could no greater trial come to Mabel, at least so she thought, than to deprive her of the pleasure of this visit; and the indulgent mamma shrunk with great pain from the task, which had been imposed upon her: yet there was no escape.

As the girls had finished breakfast and left the room before their papa went out, they of course had not heard his disagreeable intimation, and they were now in their own rooms, looking over their dresses.

'What will you do, Mabel?' inquired Julia, 'about your silk frock? You cannot possibly wear it to-day; it is quite spoiled in front with the tea. I know mamma did not notice it last night, though she and papa were so angry about your wearing it, and about the sleeves too.'

'Now just mind your own business, if you please,' said the uncourteous Mabel. 'I hear,' she added, 'that papa has gone out, so I shall go down and coax mamma to get a dress for me. I have seen plenty of pretty dresses in the shop windows, some of them very cheap; I dare say she won't object to buy me one.'

After the delivery of this speech Mabel hastily left the room, and, as she had expected, found her mamma still seated in the breakfast-room, but looking very sad.

She had not, however, at all *expected* to hear the unwelcome truth which had now to be told, and which greeted her on the first mention of a new dress.

'You need not trouble yourself about a new dress, my dear Mabel,' said her mother, sorrowfully. 'Your papa says, that he will not allow you to go with your sister to Mrs. Maitland's party.'

'Not to go!' exclaimed the astonished girl; 'and do *you*, mamma, say that I am not to go?' she inquired, actually stamping her foot in rage.

'*I* have no say in the matter, Mabel,' replied her mother; 'your papa's will must be obeyed. He thinks that it is my fault that you are so proud and wilful, and he has made up his mind to send you next week to your aunt Mary, where you will be taught and disciplined, and he hopes in time become a sensible girl, like your cousin Clara.'

'Mamma, mamma!' exclaimed the passionate girl, with vehemence, 'I hate Clara, and Aunt Mary too. I would rather die than go and live at Oak Villa, with that cross-grained old aunt and stupid cousin.'

'Mabel,' said Mrs. Ellis, greatly shocked at hearing such expressions, 'it is very wicked of you to give way to your passion, and to make such unjust remarks as you have made, both of your aunt and cousins. Neither is your aunt cross, nor your cousin Clara stupid; though cross if they were, you would still be obliged to submit to your papa's decision. Remember,' continued Mrs. Ellis, 'you have brought the trouble upon yourself, and you have been repeatedly warned of the consequences if you did not amend. Now it is too late, for I am persuaded that nothing either you or I could say would alter your papa's determination.'

A passionate burst of tears was all the reply that the humbled, but not penitent, Mabel, could make. She sat herself down on a low stool, and covering her face with her hands, continued to cry and sob, in spite of the kind remonstrances of her mamma, and even of her promises to intercede for her. Mabel knew that what her mother had before stated was quite true, and that all intercession with papa now would be in vain; and she was too much absorbed in selfish sorrow to care anything, even if she thought anything, of the pain she was giving to her poor mother, though she well knew that any trouble of mind increased the malady with which that lady was affected. Her own mortification, her own bitter disappointment, it was the thought of these that kept the sluices of sorrow open such an unreasonable time; and when Julia, on coming into the room, went to speak some words of comfort to her sister, she received a blow on the face which made her nose bleed, though certainly it was not intended, for the passionate girl was not aware of Julia's close proximity, as she threw out her hand only to indicate that she wanted no condolence.

This accident, however, had the beneficial effect, for a time, of turning the current of Mabel's ideas from self. She was indeed shocked to see what she had done, though kind-hearted Julia made light of the blow, and declared it did not pain her at all.

'I am sure you must all hate me—I think everybody hates me,' cried impetuous Mabel; 'but I didn't mean to hurt you, Julia, and I am very, very sorry for what I have done.'

'Oh, I know you are,' replied her sister; 'don't think anything more about it. And don't cry any more, dear; I can't bear to see you cry;' and she added in a whisper, 'It makes mamma ill.'

This little episode had done more to convince Mrs. Ellis of the wisdom of her husband's plan, with regard to his daughter Mabel, than all that he had said previously on the subject; and she made up her mind to offer no opposition to anything he might propose. Coming to this conclusion, she dismissed Mabel and Julia, under the plea that it was absolutely necessary that she should remain quiet for a time.

Mrs. Perring

# CHAPTER IX

## THE JUVENILE PARTY

The morning after the visit to the Gardens was temptingly fine; and at breakfast-time, Harry Maitland proposed a trip to the Kew Gardens, where, he said, there would be no fear of monkey tricks, and they would have the satisfaction of seeing specimens of the famous blue gum tree.

'But you have forgotten, I think,' said his cousin Dora, 'that we are expecting two of your school-fellows and their two sisters; Mabel and Julia Ellis, and the vicar's son and daughter, Robert and Edith Newland.'

'Oh yes, I had quite forgotten the party,' replied Harry; 'I beg everybody's pardon for being so careless. I will do as you suggest, aunt, and help Dora and Annie to prepare for the guests.'

'Thank you, my dear,' said Mrs. Maitland; 'I shall be glad to avail myself of your services, especially as I hear your cousins wish to have tea on the lawn, where there will be plenty of room for you to display your taste. I am only sorry that our good neighbour Miss Livesay, and her niece Clara, have not yet come home; so that we shall not have the pleasure of their company.'

'O, we are all very sorry on that account,' said Dora, 'for there is no one like Aunt Mary, as we call her, for making everybody feel happy and joyful. We call her the *sunbeam*,' added Dora; 'and Clara Beaumont we call the *evening star*, she is so gentle and quiet, though she is quicker at her lessons than we are, a great deal.'

'I remember Clara,' said Harry Maitland; 'poor girl, I think she was in mourning for her father when I was here in the winter. I thought she was a very nice girl, and I too am sorry that she won't be here this afternoon.'

'I believe Miss Livesay is expected home to-morrow,' said Mrs. Maitland, 'so you will have an opportunity of meeting with both her and her niece, Harry; but now, young people, you must set yourself to work, for I have many things to arrange in household matters, and can have nothing to do with decoration. Fruits and flowers, festoons and garlands, I leave entirely in your hands; I have the fullest confidence in your taste,' added the lady, laughing, and bidding them good-morning, and wishing them all success in their delightful occupation.

The Laurels, or Laurel Villa, as it was sometimes called, was a most desirable residence. Exactly like Oak Villa, its next-door neighbour, in size and appearance, so far as the house was concerned; but the gardens differed very materially, Mr. Maitland's being so well stocked, or so over-stocked with laurels, that they had actually given a name to the pleasant abode.

We won't complain of them, for they formed a delightful shade to many a rustic seat in the large back garden, and kept quite secluded the front of the house. The breakfast-room, which was at the back part of the house, opened on to the lawn with large folding glass doors; over which the balcony

Mrs. Perring

of the drawing-room formed a pleasant and very convenient shade in the summer season, at which time it rejoiced in a profusion of sweet-scented clematis, whose delicate tendrils hung luxuriantly over the balustrade, and in some places even swept the gravel walk.

The balcony itself was filled with choice flowers, and was attended to with great care, by the lady of the villa herself. The wall surrounding the garden was almost hidden by the profusion of laurels, and half a dozen rather tall trees at the bottom of the garden formed a picturesque background to the whole. The smooth-shaven lawn must not be unmentioned; it made a delightful promenade; it had been the scene of many a joyous party, and it was to be the arena on which the young invited guests of to-day were to bear witness to the artistic taste, as well as to do justice to the profusion of good things provided by their kind entertainers.

'I hope Maurice Firman won't play any of his foolish pranks to-day,' said Harry. 'He is always getting into trouble at school, yet the boys like him because he is so good-natured, and so ready to help them with their lessons; he seems as if he could not keep out of mischief. Edward is quite a different fellow, and his sisters, Ella and Lucy, are very nice girls; but they always seem afraid of Maurice, he is so fond of practical jokes.'

'I hope he won't play any while he is here,' said Dora. 'I was going to ask mamma to let us have her gold and purple cups and saucers, but if Maurice Firman is so mischievous, they might be broken.'

'Oh, as to that,' said Harry, 'I don't suppose he would attack the tea equipage, though he is a very good hand at clearing bread-and-butter plates,' he added, laughing; 'and I expect if that Miss Mabel Ellis comes, that we shall have a scene, for he is sure to turn her into ridicule.'

'Oh, I hope he wouldn't be so rude,' said Annie Maitland; 'surely he knows better how to behave himself when he is in company, and where there are young ladies?'

'I am not at all sure of him, Cousin Annie,' said Harry; 'but I do hope that silly conceited girl will not be here, to put Maurice to the test.'

'I really don't think that she will come,' said Dora; 'her papa appeared to be so angry about her going with us yesterday, that she told me that he perhaps would not give his consent to her being of our party to-day.'

'Well done, Mr. Ellis!' said Harry. 'Keep the young lady at home; we can do much better without than with her.'

'But Julia, I am sure, will not like to come without her sister,' said Annie. 'I don't think she would enjoy herself, if Mabel were not here.'

'Ah, you judge other people's feelings by your own, my kind cousin,' said the patronising Harry; 'you mustn't always do that, though I believe there is some truth in what you say about Julia Ellis.'

A silvery laugh ringing from the balcony just then made the young party look up, when they saw Mrs. Maitland, who was busy watering and rearranging her flowers, and who had been amused at her nephew's sententious speech.

'Doesn't Harry lay down the law well, mamma?' inquired Dora. 'I think,' she added, 'he will make a good barrister; he is beginning to practise so early.'

'I hope he will *practise*, as well as preach,' replied his aunt, laughing; 'example, you know, my dear boy, is better than precept,' she added, addressing herself to Harry.

'But we boys and girls require both, aunt; and I and my cousins ought to be very good, for I am sure we have both,' said the polite young gentleman, with a bow.

'At present you are all that I could wish you, my dears,' replied Mrs. Maitland; 'and I can only say now, "Go on and prosper."'

'Mamma, mamma dear, don't go just this minute,' cried Dora, as Mrs. Maitland was retreating through the drawing-room window; 'Harry has a favour to ask of you.'

'Well, what is it, Mr. Special Pleader?' inquired the lady, resuming her place on the balcony.

'Now, aunt,' said Harry, laughing, 'I don't think it is quite fair of my cousins to *engage* me in such a trifling matter, especially as I am not likely to get anything for my *brief*, except perhaps a rebuke from you.'

'Well, go on, my good sir,' said his aunt; 'I have some curiosity to learn what you have to do in the Court of Request to-day.'

'It is simply this,' replied Harry; 'my instructions are to plead for the loan of the purple and gold tea equipage, in order to make a magnificent display before the astonished eyes of a parcel of school girls and boys. That's my case, madam,' added the juvenile pleader, with a bow. 'I beg to say,' he added, after a moment's pause, 'that *I* am no advocate in this cause; I leave it entirely in the judge's hands.'

'Yes, we leave it in your hands, mamma,' said both the girls; 'we think we have confided our case to a very one-sided lawyer, and that one side is certainly against his clients.'

'I am sorry to say "no" to any petition you make, my dears,' said the kind lady; 'but prudence forbids my granting your request to-day, as misfortunes will happen, and are very likely to happen, where such a young gentleman as you describe Master Maurice Firman to be is of the party. Besides, I really think myself,' added prudent mamma, 'that the white and green tea service, though not so gorgeous as purple and gold, will be much more suitable for your present entertainment.'

'All right, aunt,' 'All right, dear mamma,' was the response to this decision.

Fortunately, in Mrs. Maitland's family, what mamma said was always right with her daughters, and this saved a world of trouble.

The happy trio went on with their preparations, and when the table was brought out on to the lawn, and had received not only the pure white and green tea-service, but the very elegant floral decorations invented by the cousins, it really had a most imposing appearance, and was pronounced by the highest authority to be perfect.

'Well, now we have prepared the feast, or at least adorned it,' said Harry, 'I think we had better look after our own adornment, for we don't appear to be in a very fit state to receive visitors—at least I can answer for myself that I am not;' and he held up his hands in proof of this affirmation, though it was evident that Dora and Annie needed no such proof, as they were pretty much in the same condition.

The young people had performed their ablutions, and were together again on the grass plot admiring their own handiwork, or rearranging here and there leaf or fern-wreath, when a ringing at the bell sounded an arrival, and Harry and his cousins met and saluted their young friends, the Firmans, in the hall: two very nice-looking girls and their two brothers, Maurice and Edward, of whom my readers have heard before.

'You will take the young gentlemen into the garden with you, dear Harry,' said Mrs. Maitland, who had come out of the dining-room to salute the guests, 'and Dora and Annie will go with the young ladies to the bedroom.'

'Mamma thinks, Mrs. Maitland,' said the eldest Miss Firman, whose name was Lucy, 'that we are too large a party to come of one family; she is afraid of giving you trouble.'

'Not in the least, my dear Lucy,' replied the kind lady. 'I wonder,' she added, 'what your mamma would say if she knew that we turned you out of doors as soon as you came.'

Lucy looked up inquiringly, and Dora explained laughingly:

'Mamma means, Lucy, that we are all going to drink tea out of doors.'

'Oh, that *will* be delightful!' exclaimed both Lucy and Ella, as they followed their young friends upstairs to remove their hats and jackets; Harry having done as his aunt had suggested, taken Maurice and Edward down the steps into the garden in the meantime. The young gentleman was well aware that he had rather a rough customer to deal with in Master Maurice, as he had more than once been the object of his school-fellow's practical jokes; so he thought proper to give him a caution.

'Now, I say, Maurice,' began Harry Maitland, 'don't let's have any of your school-boy tricks here, that's a good fellow; you know we have young ladies to deal with this afternoon, and we must try to please them.'

'Oh, I'm not going to do anything foolish; don't be afraid, old fellow,' said his companion. 'Why, Harry, you look as solemn as though you expected me to fly away with the tea-table and all the good things upon it,' he remarked, as he glanced with a well-satisfied and complacent look at the said tea-table; and added, 'I assure you that I don't mean to do anything so shocking, but shall content myself with a moderate share of the excellent provisions with which it is stocked.'

This speech was delivered with mock gravity, and our friend Harry was fain to be satisfied with the promise, as the young ladies just then made their appearance, and there was a very general exclamation of pleasure and admiration at the really pretty and tasteful surroundings.

Another ring at the bell announced more visitors, and the good vicar's children, Robert and Edith Newlove, made their appearance on the top of the steps, and soon joined the rest in their admiration of what had been effected by the artistic efforts of their young friends. Harry cordially greeted his school companion and especial favourite, Robert Newlove, while Dora and Annie welcomed with a kiss his gentle sister Edith; and soon the happy party were seated round the table, where Dora was to preside, though she had much wished that her mamma should take that important office upon herself.

'I thought you told me that Mabel and Julia Ellis were to be here, Dora,' said Edith Newlove, who was seated near her friend. 'Are they not coming?' she inquired.

'I really don't know how it will be,' replied Dora, quietly, for she did not wish to attract notice. 'Julia I hope will be here soon, but I fear Mabel will not be permitted to come; her papa is very much displeased with her.'

Another ring at the bell made the young party suspend operations for a few minutes, and Julia Ellis received a cordial welcome, and soon found a seat near Harry Maitland, who had risen to receive her.

Maurice Firman, not wishing to be less courteous than his friend Harry, had also risen from his seat, but very unfortunately—or shall I say clumsily?—in doing so, the contents of his cup went over on to his trousers, and he was too much engaged in keeping off the hot beverage from touching his skin, to deal in matters of courtesy.

'What a clumsy fellow you are, Maurice,' said his brother Edward; 'always getting into hot water.'

'Oh, don't bother!' exclaimed Maurice, petulantly, and still shaking his trousers. 'I'd rather get into hot water than have the hot water poured upon me;' and having said, as he thought, a witty thing, and made the whole party laugh (which I must confess they had all been very much inclined to do before at his expense), he seated himself again at the table, cooling down as the hot beverage had done, and trying to make himself agreeable to his young friends by his very lively remarks, of which he had a good store.

'Why is your sister Mabel not with you, Julia?' inquired Lucy Firman. 'I hope she is not unwell?' she added, seeing the colour rise on the cheeks of the poor girl.

'Mrs. Ellis is not very well,' replied Dora Maitland, answering for her friend; while Harry, in order to check further inquiries, asked Maurice Firman if he had ever been to the Zoological Gardens.

'I should just think I had,' replied Maurice, with a very significant shake of the head; 'but you won't catch me there again in a hurry. Why, I tumbled over into the bear's den, or cage, or whatever you call it; and if Master Bruin had been at the bottom of the pole, instead of the top, I can't tell you where my poll would have been now. Fortunately, the keeper was there, and I was got out somehow or other, I can't tell you how, for I was insensible when they picked me up; and that was no wonder, for I think I could not have been very *sensible* when I tumbled over. When I came round I found myself lying on my own bed, and mamma, and the doctor, and the girls all crying: no, the doctor wasn't crying—doctors never do cry, I suppose, it is beneath their dignity; but the others made fuss enough, and it was nearly a month before I was able to go out again. And depend upon it, when I did go out, I didn't walk to the Zoological Gardens, for I can't bear the name of the place.' Maurice doubtless thought that he had made a good hit, but alas! it only fell on one pair of ears.

Fortunately the tea passed over without any other mishap than the upsetting of the cup. Maurice Firman was certainly the chief spokesman of the party; and though I am compelled to admit that he displayed great attachment for plates of cake and bread and butter, I am also bound in justice to say that he was not at all wanting in courtesy to the young ladies, by whom he was surrounded. Everything, indeed, was pleasant, and as it should be, and the now antiquated game of croquet was proposed, as soon as the table with its adjuncts could be removed.

'Now I'll toss this ball, and catch it ten times running, with one hand, while you are waiting for your game,' cried the impatient Maurice; and though there was a general exclamation of 'No, no, not until the table is cleared!' away went the ball into the air, and returned safely into the hand that sent it.

The next descent, however, was a disastrous one, for the ball fell exactly in the middle of the table, smashing more than one of the bread-and-butter plates, to the great distress and consternation of the whole party.

'Oh, how fortunate it is that we had not the best china tea-things,' said Dora; 'they are very expensive ones. It does not matter much about these; we can easily get them matched.'

'Well, I am *very very* sorry,' said the author of the mischief; 'but I'll save up all my pocket-money, and buy some more plates,' he added.

'No, no, you won't,' said a kind voice from the balcony; and on Maurice looking up, he saw Mrs. Maitland, who had come out of the drawing-room to ascertain the cause of the commotion. 'Don't let this trifling accident spoil your sport, dear Maurice,' said the lady, smiling on the impetuous yet generous-hearted boy; 'only take care that you do not hurt your young friends, the ladies, by too rough play.' Having given this necessary caution, Mrs. Maitland left them to their sports, and as the unfortunate breakage had been the means of checking somewhat of the exuberant spirits of the youthful offender, everything went on very satisfactorily, and game succeeded game, with great amiability, until an unfortunate cat, belonging to Aunt Mary, which had accustomed itself to take an evening's promenade along the garden wall, made her usual appearance, and attracted the attention of the mischief-loving Maurice.

'Oh, I must have a fling at that cat,' cried that young gentleman, taking up a rather thick piece of stick from the bushes. 'Now see if I don't hit her right down from the wall,' he added; and he was just going to suit the action to the word, when he felt his arms pinioned from behind, and tried in vain to make his escape.

The cat, however, was more fortunate, for seeing that she had attracted attention, and very likely having had some acquaintance with school-boy tricks, she very prudently contented herself with a short walk this evening, and quietly slipped down into her own domain before the pinioned arms were set at liberty.

'There, now you may go, old fellow,' said Harry Maitland, releasing the arms, which he had held so tightly that Maurice was fain to rub them violently to restore the circulation, while the whole party laughed heartily at his expense.

'I wish Harry was at home with you sometimes,' said Edward Firman, who did not seem at all to relish his boisterous ways.

'I wish he was,' replied Maurice, who looked rather red and angry at having been so ignominiously made captive. 'But you don't think,' he added, 'that I would let him master me so easily as he has done now, Ned; I was taken unawares, and that's not fair.'

'But that was the only way to save the poor cat,' said Dora Maitland: 'she might have been killed if you had struck her with that large piece of wood; and I think Cousin Harry did quite right in holding your arms.'

'Such a fuss about a cat!' cried Maurice, still smarting under the supposed affront. 'You should see how I served one the other day, when she came prowling about the house to steal anything she could lay hold of.'

'Don't let him tell—don't let him tell it, 'cried both Lucy and Ethel Firman; 'it is a great shame of you, Maurice, to boast of your own bad deeds,' said both his sisters; and as the servants were just then again setting out the table with refreshments, the young party were saved the infliction of hearing an exploit boasted of, which would certainly have lowered Maurice Firman considerably in the eyes of all present.

'I did not intend to hurt you, Maurice,' said Harry Maitland, as he clapped his friend on the back, and held out his hand in token of amity.

'Oh, I know that,' replied the boy; 'I shouldn't play tricks with cats where there are girls.'

'Nor at all, I think,' responded his friend; 'it is a cowardly thing to hurt a dumb creature that cannot speak or fight for itself.'

'Can't they, though!' cried Maurice; 'I know, if they don't speak, they can make a horrible outcry. And as to fighting, just look here, my boy, what do you think of that for a scratch, which a wretch of a cat gave me because I took up her kitten and made it squall? Why, she flew at me like mad, and before I could put the kitten down, she gave me this wound;' and Maurice uncovered his wrist, and showed a very red and angry-looking scratch.

'It's your own fault; you should let the cats alone,' said his sisters. 'Mamma is always scolding you for teasing them.'

'Well, I think we have had enough of cats,' said Robert Newlove; 'I don't like them myself, but I should be very sorry to hurt them;' and in this charitable declaration he was seconded by the whole party, Maurice excepted.

We must now bid good-night to our young friends, as they will soon do to each other. Aunt Mary and Clara are expected home to-morrow, and that careful domestic of hers, Bridget Morley, who has lived so many years at Oak Villa, has got everything in apple-pie order for her much-esteemed mistress, and a lovely brood of chickens, which have been hatched since they went away, to present to the young lady who has the charge of all the poultry.

# CHAPTER X

## THE BROKEN BOX

Before we congratulate ourselves on Aunt Mary's return home, let us just take a look at the disappointed Mabel, after her sister Julia had gone to the tea-party.

It was in vain that her too indulgent mother tried to soften her affliction, very injudiciously, we think, as every remark of hers only elicited a fresh burst of feeling; and Mrs. Ellis felt it quite a relief when the self-tormenting girl rose up hastily and retreated to her bedroom, there to ponder over, not her own delinquencies, we fear, but the wrongs inflicted on her by others.

A little voice which said, 'May I come in, Mabel?' roused her for a moment, and she answered very crossly: 'What is it you want, Fred? I wish you would not come teasing me. Go away; I don't want any of you.

'I only want to show you the nice box of puzzles papa has brought home for me,' replied Freddy. 'I want you, Mabel dear, to help me to put it together. I won't tease you.'

'I don't want to see your box, and I shan't open the door,' said the ungracious girl. 'Take your box away, and get some one else to help you to put your puzzle together,' she added; and poor Fred, thus rudely repressed, turned to wend his way downstairs again. Unfortunately, his foot caught the fringe of the door-mat, which caused him to fall heavily and strike his head against the railing of the banisters, while the pretty box, escaping from his hand, went right down the stairs into the hall, where it burst open, and scattered the inclosed pieces right and left.

Mabel was now quite roused, and fearing that her papa, attracted by the noise, might come up to see what was the matter, rather than being moved by any sisterly feeling, she reluctantly opened the door, and lifted up the prostrate Freddy, who, although he had received a rather severe blow on the forehead from coming in contact with the railings, was too much of a man to cry, and seemed more anxious about the fate of his new plaything, than desirous of obtaining either aid or sympathy; nor was he very likely to obtain either from Mabel, though she took him into her room to scold him for what he had done.

'Now just see what you have done,' said the selfish girl, 'by bringing up that nasty box, and then letting it fall down the stairs. I hear papa's voice in the hall; he will most likely come up here, and I shall get scolded for your stupidity.'

'I will go down to him,' said Freddy, 'and then I can tell him all about the box falling; papa needn't come up here.'

'How came you to let your box fall, Fred?' inquired Mr. Ellis, helping the boy to pick up the scattered pieces.

'I caught my foot in the fringe of the bedroom mat, papa,' replied Freddy; 'I am so sorry the box is broken.'

'Yes, so am I,' said his father; 'but why did you take it

upstairs? that is what I should like to know.'

As there was no answer returned to this question, Mr. Ellis stated the truth himself.

'I suppose,' he continued, 'you went to show it to your sister Mabel—was that it?'

'Yes, papa,' said the boy, still holding down his head; and kind papa, seeing there was something wrong, would not then press further questions on his little boy, though he remarked to his wife, when they were again seated, that he should indeed be very glad when Mabel was under the care of someone who knew how to manage her, for he was quite disgusted with her exhibitions of temper.

'My sister will I dare say be here to-morrow,' said Mrs. Ellis; 'and I will tell her what you wish respecting Mabel, though I know she does not like the poor girl: and Mabel will find Oak Villa very different to home, I am afraid.'

'That is not what I am afraid of,' replied Mr. Ellis; 'my fear is, that Miss Livesay will find the girl so intolerable, that we shall soon have her back on our hands again.'

'Oh, Arthur! you are so very severe in your remarks,' said the too indulgent mother. 'My sister is very patient, and very kind to children, though she is so firm.'

'Which I am sorry to say you are not, my dear; and it is this want of firmness which occasions all the mischief,' said the gentleman; adding, rather bitterly, 'You order a thing to be done, but you take no care to see your orders enforced, and thus we are plagued with unruly children and wilful servants.'

'Well, dear, you are always finding fault with me, whatever I do,' said the poor self-afflicted lady, though she must have felt that what her good husband had said was quite true; and well would it have been for him, for herself, and indeed for the whole household, if, instead of considering herself a martyr, she had set to work to amend the errors which he had pointed out; but, alas! we don't see ourselves as others see us.

# CHAPTER XI

## AUNT MARY'S RETURN

On the evening of the day after the juvenile party, a cab drove up to the garden gate of Oak Villa, and Dora and Annie Maitland, who had been on the look-out for some time at the window of an upper room, had the satisfaction of seeing their kind preceptress, and her niece Clara Beaumont, alight from it, receiving and giving at the same time the welcome nod and smile of recognition. But here is the trusty Bridget, with her merry face beaming with gladness, and her voice almost tremulous with joy, for she has had rather a dull time of it while her mistress and Clara have been away; though Jane Somers, a young girl living not far off from Oak Villa, came regularly to sleep at the house.

'Well, Bridget, and how have you been all this time? not idle, I can see at the first glance,' said Aunt Mary, looking round at the brightly-polished furniture and fire-irons.

'Oh no, ma'am, I don't think anybody can be idle at your house,' replied Bridget; 'and I have had plenty to do, for I have cleaned the house from top to bottom, and have taken care of the cat and the fowls. And oh, Miss Clara, the old hen has brought out such a beautiful set of chickens as you never seed afore; but I dare say you be too tired to come and look at them now,' added Bridget.

'Yes, we are too tired now,' said Miss Livesay, answering for her niece; 'we want to take off our wraps, and have some tea. Besides, you forget, my good woman,' added her mistress, 'that the chickens are now all hidden under their mother's wing, and she wouldn't suffer us to disturb them.'

'Dear me, I quite forgot that,' said Bridget, as she busied herself in assisting in the removal of cloaks and shawls, and carrying off trunks and band-boxes; one of the latter of which her kind mistress told her was for her, and contained a new cap and bonnet.

'Oh, ma'am, you are so kind,' said the pleased domestic; 'you never forget anyone.' And she hurried away with her load, with a glad tear glistening in her eye.

It was quite true what Bridget had said about Aunt Mary— she was indeed kind-hearted and open-handed: but with all this she was not foolishly indulgent. Her judgment was correct, and having made up her mind as to what was the right course to pursue, she took pains to see her plans carried out. Often and often had she remonstrated with her sister, Mrs. Ellis, on her laxity of discipline, both with her children and servants; and sometimes she had ventured, though that perhaps was not very wise, to set their mutual friend Mrs. Maitland before her as a pattern for mothers and mistresses. This, however, invariably produced some angry retort, or at least a flood of tears, and ended with a secret determination on the part of the elder sister to say no more on the subject, but permit things to take their course; though she had made up her mind on coming home to do as Mr. Ellis had once suggested to her, that was, to receive Mabel as one of her pupils.

This was entirely with the idea of relieving her sister, and effecting a reformation, if possible, in the character of her niece; though she almost dreaded the introduction of such an element of discord into their peaceful and happy household. Mabel, we have seen, had a great dislike to her gentle cousin Clara, perhaps because she had heard her praises often sounded; and she disliked her Aunt Mary quite as much, though it would have been difficult for her to have given a 'reason why,' if it had been asked for.

'I shall hate them both, I know I shall,' said Mabel to her sister Julia, on the morning of the day on which Miss Livesay was expected to come to Camden Terrace. 'There will be lessons and work, lessons and work, all the day long. I shall be miserable, I know I shall; and I'll tell mamma so, and beg of her not to let me go.'

'No, don't do that, Mabel; you will only make poor mamma unhappy, and papa angry,' said the wise younger sister; and she added, 'I wish I could go to Oak Villa. I like Cousin Clara very much, and Dora and Annie Maitland too; I am sure you will find them very nice companions, all of them.'

'Oh yes, it's all very fine what you are saying,' said Mabel; 'but I know very well that you only want to get rid of me, and so does papa, for I heard him say so; and I think it's unkind and cruel of you both,' exclaimed the angry girl.

'Well, at any rate, you are not going very far away from us,' said Julia; 'it is only a nice walk from Oak Villa to our house, so I and Freddy can come and see you often, and you can come to see us.'

Just then a cab was heard to stop at the door, and the dreaded lady and her niece Clara alighted, each with parcels in their hands; presents, no doubt, to the small fry who had climbed up to the window to see who was coming.

'Now don't look so cross, Mabel; don't let Aunt Mary see that you don't like to go to Oak Villa,' entreated Julia.

'But I shall let her see!' replied the perverse girl; 'and I *shall* tell her so, too—see if I don't,' she added, nodding her head; though, when she came into the presence of that good lady, she had not a word to say for herself, such a charm is there in the manner of some people to overawe presumption.

Mabel and Julia made their appearance in the dining-room, just after the first kindly greetings and affectionate salutations of the sisters had been exchanged, and the same process had to be gone over with cousins and aunt, the latter showing no difference whatever in the warm embrace of Mabel and Julia, though we well know the great difference there was in her estimate of the character of the two girls.

'Well, my dear Mabel,' said Miss Livesay, after a little conference had been held, 'so it appears your papa and mamma wish that we should become better acquainted with each other. Shall you like to pay me a visit at Oak Villa?'

Here was a grand opportunity for Mabel to display her boasted courage, and to speak her mind; instead of which, she only looked very sad, hung down her head, and, rudely enough, made no reply; while her aunt said, with a smile:

'That is well; silence gives consent. So you had better go, my dear, and get ready, for I do not wish to keep the cabman waiting; and I have just a few words to say to your mamma. Clara and Julia will therefore go upstairs with you.'

All this was said kindly, but very decidedly: it was evident that there was no appeal to be made, no authority to be questioned; and with hardly suppressed passion and tears, the vanquished girl quitted the room with her sister and cousin.

'And now, my dear Ada,' said Miss Livesay to her sister, 'see what are the fruits of your over-indulgence, or want of firmness! They are not very lovely, are they? Will you not take your good husband's advice, and strive against this constitutional weakness, which is so detrimental to your happiness, to your husband's comfort, and to your children's welfare?'

'I can't be always scolding the children, Mary,' replied Mrs. Ellis, peevishly. 'It isn't my fault, surely, that Mabel is so ill-tempered and disobedient, and yet you and Arthur just talk to me as if it were.'

'And in a great measure, I think, it is your fault, my sister,' said the kind monitor. 'Children should be watched from infancy; tenderly cared for in mind as well as body. Good seed must be sown then, and the little weeds which we are apt to disregard, or what is worse, cherish, in our folly, must be rooted out while the soil is moist, and the root is not deep in the ground. Never laugh at childish exhibitions of temper, nor for the sake of *peace* give way to the doctrine of *expediency*, injurious alike to nations and to families.'

Here poor Mrs. Ellis interposed; she could never sit out a long sermon, especially one that she really could not understand. So she interrupted Aunt Mary's profitable discourse by promising to try, when Mabel had gone away, to be more careful for the future, though she candidly admitted that she did not know how to begin to make any change, as Mabel was the only one of the children who gave her any trouble. And yet the weeds were growing up thick and strong in Master Freddy, who just then put his head in at the door, the little ones being behind him, and all running to salute their aunt, and receiving from her a loving embrace, as well as the very pretty playthings which were spread out on the table for their acceptance and admiration. Nor had Mabel and Julia been forgotten by their aunt; both a workbox and a writing-case were laid aside for the latter: those intended for her sister Miss Livesay had not brought, thinking it unnecessary, as Mabel was to return with her to Oak Villa.

'Well, my dear Mabel,' said Aunt Mary, as the two girls entered the room; 'so you are equipped and ready for a start, I see. I do hope you will like your new mode of life, and your young companion's society. Clara, I know, will be delighted to have a companion in her visits to our poor people: and you, I trust, will soon learn to take an interest in them.'

There was no response to this kind speech from the unamiable girl; and with the somewhat painful feeling on the part of Miss Livesay that she was going to introduce into her hitherto peaceful household the apple of discord, she rose to take leave, with the promise, however, of renewing her visit in the next week if all things went on well.

Mabel was quick enough to notice this speech: she would have known that it had reference to herself, even if it had not been accompanied by a smile and a nod from her aunt; and the naughty pride in her heart made her resent it, though she felt obliged to submit.

There were loving adieus from all but Master Freddy, who said to his sister, as she shook hands with him:

'Good-bye, Mabel; I'm glad you're going, you are always so cross with us.'

# CHAPTER XII

## NIGHT AND MORNING

And now an entirely new mode of life was presented to Mabel; and Miss Livesay found, as, indeed, she had expected to find, a fruitful source of trouble in her newly adopted pupil. Of course, on the first day of Mabel's arrival at Oak Villa there were no lessons talked about, and the young ladies next door were not expected to resume their school duties, until the Monday following Miss Livesay's return home; so there was a little time afforded for breaking *out*, and breaking *in*. We shall see how it was employed.

This afternoon had been a very pleasant one; the chickens had been looked at and greatly admired; flowers, the great favourites both of aunt and niece, Mabel did not care for, though she liked, as we have seen, to deck herself in gay colours. In the house they had plenty of amusement, with books and pretty specimens of work of various kinds from the ready fingers and artistic taste of Aunt Mary and Clara; indeed, what had been produced by their skill, industry, and steady perseverance, was worthy of admiration. To Mabel's astonishment, nine o'clock struck, and she had not yet finished her pleasant occupation of examining, when her aunt said:

'Now, my dears, it is your bed-time.'

Clara instantly began to put away books and work, but Mabel exclaimed:

'Oh, aunt! must we go to bed so soon? I never go till ten, at home!'

'Perhaps you never rise at six in the morning?' replied Miss Livesay; 'we do. And I dare say you have heard the old proverb—

"'Early to bed, and early to rise,
Is the way to be healthy, wealthy, and wise."'

'I go to bed when I like, and I get up when I like, at home,' said Mabel, without noticing the unwelcome quotation.

'*We* have no *likes* and *dislikes* here, my dear Mabel,' said her aunt. 'We do what we know to be our duty, and you will have to do the same. Good-night!'

An affectionate kiss accompanied the *good-night*; Mabel saw that it was a *decided* one; there was no room for further parley, and the short time spent by the proud and petulant girl at Oak Villa gave signs of an authority, to which she must of necessity submit, as from it there could be no appeal.

'Mabel dear, it is time to get up; don't you hear the bell ringing?' said Clara, as she jumped out of bed and began to dress. The sleepy-headed girl turned lazily round, but did not seem to be at all disposed to attend to the summons.

'You *must* get up; indeed you must!' urged Clara, gently shaking her cousin by the shoulder. 'I shall not have done all I have to do before prayers, if we don't make haste.'

'Why, what have we to do before breakfast? And what time do you have breakfast?' drowsily inquired Mabel, rising, however, at this second appeal of her cousin's.

'We have prayers at eight, then breakfast; but I have my chickens to feed, and my lessons to prepare before that time,' said Clara.

'Lessons before breakfast! Oh, I shall hate that!' exclaimed Mabel. 'I hope they are not hard ones, for I shall never learn them if they are.'

'Well, I don't know what you call hard,' replied her cousin. 'I find mine rather difficult sometimes, but Aunt Mary is so kind in explaining everything, that it is quite a pleasure to learn with her.'

'I'm sure I shouldn't think her kind,' said the ungrateful Mabel. 'I can't bear people that are so prim and stiff as Aunt Mary is, always seeming determined to make you do just what they like, whether you wish it or not.'

'Oh, Mabel!' said her cousin, 'I wonder how you can speak so disrespectfully of dear Aunt Mary; and what you are saying is quite untrue.'

'And I suppose,' retorted the ill-conditioned girl, 'you will go and tell her what I have said, and we shall have a row.'

Clara was so astonished at hearing this speech from her cousin, that she suspended the operation of dressing for a moment.

Then she said quickly:

'Mabel, we don't tell tales here; and I never before heard

anyone speak unkindly of our aunt, nor did I ever hear her speak unkindly to anyone. Don't let us talk any more,' she added; 'I am going to say my prayers. Come, kneel down with me, and let us thank our Father in heaven for taking care of us through the night, and ask Him to bless us before we begin our day's work.'

Mabel knelt down beside the bed with her cousin. She had always been accustomed to repeat a set form of words; whether they were the utterances of the 'soul's sincere desire,' we cannot say: but we do know that if we *pray* in sincerity against sin, we shall *strive* against it, and Mabel was not doing this. Clara's first occupation on going down stairs was to look after her feathered family; and in this she had a ready seconder in Mabel, whose delight in seeing the pretty chickens was unbounded.

'Oh, do let me take one out, Clara! I won't hurt it; dear, sweet little thing!' she exclaimed, as she was just putting out her hand to take one of them up, but was held back by her cousin, and so prevented from receiving the meditated peck which the old hen was evidently preparing for her.

'Just in time,' said Clara; 'old Netty would have made you repent of your boldness, had you taken hold of one of her pets.'

'Why, I shouldn't have hurt it by just holding it in my hand,' replied Mabel.

'Netty doesn't know that; and I'm sure she would have hurt you, so it is very well I held you back,' said Clara. 'Now we had better go in; I hear Aunt Mary's voice. I must go and say good-morning to her, as usual.'

'Good-morning, my dears,' said Miss Livesay, in her usual

genial, happy tone of voice, for she was always bright and cheerful, though her niece Mabel chose to take such a distorted view of her. 'I hope you have slept well, and are refreshed for another day's work, my children; you both look the picture of health, and health is one of our greatest blessings, is it not?'

'Yes, dear aunt, indeed it is,' replied Clara. 'I think we both slept well; and I was so glad to see, when I woke, that the morning was fine, for I thought perhaps you would wish us to go and see how poor Mr. Simmons is, when we have done our lessons.'

'That is just what I wish you to do,' said Aunt Mary. 'The lessons I intend to postpone, except that you may show your cousin what you and your school-fellows are learning. I shall be delighted to find that you can all study together; it will save much time and trouble, and be much more agreeable. Now ring for Bridget; after prayers and breakfast, we must cut out our work, dear Clara. You know we have a great deal to do,' said the lady.

# CHAPTER XIII

## THE FIRST DAY'S WORK

IN the pleasant breakfast-room, which was also a schoolroom, the two girls were left by Aunt Mary, while she gave some orders on household matters. Everything was arranged here with order and neatness, but there was nothing superfluous; there was a place for everything, and everything seemed to be in its place, if we except a large quantity of unbleached calico, which had been unrolled, and had spread itself upon the floor.

'What is all that coarse stuff for?' inquired Mabel of her cousin. 'You surely don't call that your work, do you, Clara? I brought some embroidery with me, for I hate plain work. I hope aunt will not set me to do any.'

'I am quite sure she will, though,' replied Clara; 'and this very day, too; for she is going to cut out two night-shirts for the poor man we are going to see, and we shall have to make them, as well as pinafores for the children, and flannel petticoats for two old women who are in Aunt Mary's district. Oh, such nice old dames they are, Mabel! I am sure you will like them, dear; and they are so thankful for any little kindness we do for them.'

'Such stupid, humdrum work!' exclaimed Mabel. 'I'm sure I shall be miserable here. Hard lessons, coarse work, and looking after old and sick people! I wonder you are not moped to death, Clara; it's even worse than I thought it would be.'

'Well, wait a little while,' said patient Clara; 'you have had no experience yet. I know very well you will alter your mind before six months are over.'

'Six months!' exclaimed Mabel; 'why, I should be dead in that time, if mamma suffers me to remain here. But I shall tell her all about it, and beg her to let me go home.'

The entrance of Aunt Mary broke off the dialogue of the cousins, and soon the obnoxious calico was spread out, and fashioned into useful articles of wearing apparel.

'Here is your new workbox, my dear Mabel,' said her aunt; 'you will find it stocked with all necessary things—thimble, and scissors, and needles, and cotton—and all that I require of you is to keep it tidy.'

It was impossible for Mabel not to dismiss *some*, at least, of her foolish prejudice against this kind friend, and the thanks she returned for the really handsome present were hearty and genuine; and on fitting on her thimble, and examining the bright scissors and the very pretty needle, even her feelings respecting the coarse work on which they were expected to be employed appeared to undergo a wonderful change.

'I can't do plain work very quickly, aunt,' said Mabel, when that lady had given her a pair of sleeves to make; 'I never did much at home.'

'All right, my child; if you do your best, I promise you I shall be satisfied. I know you will improve in time,' said Aunt Mary, kindly.

There was no reading this morning, because Clara and Aunt Mary, who were both rapid seamstresses, had agreed, if possible, to finish the night-shirt that had been cut out, and take it with them in the evening, when they went to call at the cottage of poor Simmons, whom they had not seen since their return home, but of whom they had learned from Bridget a pretty satisfactory account. The good woman had taken them under her especial care while her mistress was away.

There was no lack of pleasant conversation when Aunt Mary was in the room, and the work progressed well during the morning hours; but, unfortunately, about three o'clock in the afternoon some friends came to call, and as it was evident to Miss Livesay that this would prevent their visit to the cottage that evening, she bade the young people put away their work, and try to find some amusement in the garden. Clara felt sorry and disappointed at this postponement, though she said nothing, but prepared to obey her aunt. With Mabel, however, this was quite an unexpected pleasure, and so rapidly did she gather up her work, without folding it neatly together, that the needle ran into her finger, and brought the blood so quickly that two or three large spots were deposited on the sleeves.

'Oh, aunt will be so cross when she sees what I have done!' said the too hasty Mabel. 'Must I try to wash the spots out, Clara?' she inquired.

'No, no!' replied her cousin; 'Bridget will do that for you with a little brush. But I wonder, Mabel,' she added, 'at your thinking dear aunt would be *cross* because you have had an accident. You seem to have some very strange ideas in your head; you will know better soon, I hope.'

The room was quickly cleared, and Clara, taking the soiled sleeve in her hand, went with her cousin into the kitchen, where they found the tidy servant-of-all-work already clean, and sitting comfortably with her knitting in hand, and the cat on her knee. Bridget readily undertook the task required of her; and the young people, having obtained the food for the poultry, ran off to distribute it.

A capital house Clara's feathered family had, with no rent nor taxes to pay. It was a long shed under the tall trees at the bottom of the garden, boarded over at the top, but with wire-work all across the front, where a door was made to go in at, in order to clean out the floor.

Inside, it was the picture of comfort, and of cleanliness too, for careful Bridget took care of that. Old Netty and her chicks had a place to themselves—a house within a house—so that the little ones could not make an escape.

'Oh, I see there are two new-laid eggs,' said Clara. 'I am so glad; we can take them to poor Simmons when we go to-morrow. I dare say there are two or three more in the house that I may have.'

'I thought you said the fowls were your own, to do what you liked with,' said Mabel. 'If I were you, I should sell the eggs, and not give them away,' she added.

'And what should I do with the money?' inquired Clara. 'I have everything I want; aunt takes care of that.'

'But you might buy nice gloves and neckties with the money you would get for the eggs,' urged Mabel. 'I don't see that you have much of that sort of thing.'

'I have all that I want in that way,' replied her cousin. 'I would ten times rather give away the eggs than take money for them. When I first came to live with dear aunt, she had this place fitted up on purpose for me; and she bought the fowls, and food, and everything that was wanted,' said Clara. 'In three months' time I had a beautiful brood of chickens; and when they were grown, aunt asked me what I meant to do with my surplus stock. I said that I really did not know; so she suggested that I should sell the chickens, and give the money to the poor. "Sell that ye have, and give alms," said my aunt. "This, dear Clara, is our Saviour's advice," she added, and I was only too glad and thankful to follow her advice. So I made a purse, in which I save up my egg-and-chicken money, and we buy calico, and print, and flannel, and provide other things,' said Clara, in great glee, for it was, indeed, one of her chief sources of pleasure to give to the poor.

'I'm sure you would not catch me doing in that way,' said Mabel. 'I see no fun in keeping fowls only for the sake of giving to other people.'

'No *fun*, perhaps,' replied her cousin; 'but you would find real pleasure, Mabel, in being able to relieve the wants of the sick and the afflicted. Oh, I know,' she added, 'you will—you *must* change your mind when you go with us to some of the neighbouring cottages. I do hope we shall not be prevented from going to-morrow.'

Whatever effect time and scenes were to have on our young friend Mabel, certainly her cousin's arguments and declarations produced none at the present; so we must close the chapter of the first day, and begin another.

# CHAPTER XIV

## VISIT TO THE COTTAGE

The evening of this first day at Oak Villa had been very pleasantly spent by Aunt Mary and her nieces at Mr. Maitland's, where the young people engaged themselves on the lawn, while the elders talked over the various events of the very eventful times, without being able to come to any conclusion as to how they were to be mended.

Mabel either really *was* in a very gracious humour this evening, or the fact of a young gentleman being of their party made her careful not to give way to temper; though it must be confessed that Harry tried it two or three times. However, all went on smoothly enough, and at nine o'clock the friends separated.

The gorgeous sunset gave token of a fine day on the morrow, when Clara anticipated the pleasure of finishing her labour of love, and taking a most acceptable present to her poor friends the Simmonses. The bell rang at the usual time in the morning, and after breakfast the work of the day before was resumed.

'Two hours, I think, will finish what you want to take with you to-day,' said Aunt Mary, 'so you will have time to go before dinner. You can take poor Simmons some eggs, and Bridget has a rice pudding in the oven for the children.'

'How delighted they will be to see us again; only I wish you could have gone with us, aunt,' said Clara.

'I wish I could have done so, but I expect a person to call on business this morning, so I must not be out of the way,' said the lady.

Steadily the work progressed; even Mabel, by the aid of her bright silver thimble and sharp needle, seemed to get on better than she had done the day before: so that not only was the night-shirt finished, but a little pinafore had been cut out and completed in less than the two hours. And now all had been packed up, the two girls were ready for their walk; and the careful Bridget had placed the pudding and the eggs in an oval basket for Clara to carry, while they were preparing for their walk.

'It will be frightfully hot walking this morning, I know,' said Mabel. 'I wish our visit to the cottage could be put off until the evening; go and ask Aunt Mary if it may, Clara,' she added.

'No, I couldn't do that,' replied her cousin. 'Aunt never tells us to do anything that is unreasonable, and I know that she wishes very much that the children should have the pudding for their dinner, and that the poor sick man should have the new-laid eggs. Come, Mabel dear, be quick,' she added; 'we shall be under the shade of the trees great part of the way.'

'And who is to carry the basket and this parcel?' inquired Mabel, giving a rather contemptuous look at the rolled-up work.

Mrs. Perring

'You may carry whichever you like,' said Clara; 'it does not matter to me which I take. Indeed, I shouldn't mind if I had to carry both, neither of them are heavy.'

'Perhaps not,' said the proud girl, 'but it is so servant-like to be carrying parcels and baskets; I wonder Aunt Mary likes you to do it.'

'Oh, Mabel!' cried her cousin, 'I can't help laughing at you. Why, you should see what bundles aunt and I do carry sometimes. I suppose you would be quite shocked.'

'I shouldn't wish to be seen with you,' replied the silly girl. 'I don't think, either, that it is any laughing matter.' And Clara, knowing that it was a waste of time to argue the case any further, took up the obnoxious bundle, and ran downstairs; while Mabel followed, to find on the hall-table her share of the disagreeable, in the closely-packed basket.

It really was a very hot walk that the cousins had before them, in spite of the occasional shade of the tall trees, and they were not at all sorry when they reached the small cottage of James Simmons, and were invited to sit and rest on the chairs, which the good wife dusted and put ready for them.

The cottage was very poorly supplied with furniture—one table, and four chairs, and a stool, on which stood the washing-tub, out of which Mrs. Simmons was wringing some clothes from very hot water, when her visitors entered. If, however, there was but little furniture, there was no lack of children, and three of them were rolling about the floor, while a girl, it might be of the age of seven, was making an attempt to wash some stockings. Her small fingers did not seem to be equal to the task of rubbing and wringing, yet she was evidently proud of her occupation—a great deal more so than her brother appeared of his, in trying to take care of the youngest child, a chubby infant of six months old, who would persist in rolling off his knee, and making towards the fireplace, there to become a regular Cinderella.

This scene, I need hardly say, was anything but delightful to the new visitor, though she did not refuse to seat herself on the offered chair; while poor Mrs. Simmons, with many apologies for being found in such a rough state, wiped her hot face with her apron, and took the little one up from the floor, to the great relief of her brother Johnny, who appeared particularly interested in the contents of the basket, which Clara was proceeding to set upon the table.

'Let me take the baby, Mrs. Simmons, while you put the eggs into a basin; I am afraid of their rolling off the table,' said Clara, as she held out her arms to take the very pretty, but certainly not very clean little one.

'Oh, miss! she is not in a fit state for you to nurse,' replied the woman; 'I am quite ashamed that you should have found us all so dirty, but indeed I cannot help it. What with my husband being ill so long, and the washing, which must be done, I don't know sometimes which way to turn.'

'My aunt wants much to know how your husband is,' said Clara; 'she would have come with us this morning, but she had an engagement.'

'The doctor thinks, miss, that my husband may get well, though he says it may be many weeks yet before he will be able to walk. He has had a weary time of it, and if it had not been for Miss Livesay's kindness, and that of our good vicar and his wife, I think he could not have lived; for he required more nourishment than I could obtain for him, if I worked ever so hard.'

Mrs. Perring

'I know how glad my aunt will be to hear this good news,' said Clara; 'and she has sent one of the night-shirts that we have made; I dare say she will bring the other herself. And now let me try on the pinafore for baby; I want to see whether it will fit.' Baby, however, stoutly resisted this trial, using arms and legs with marvellous dexterity, and almost twisting herself out of mother's arms; so the contest was given up for fear of creating a noise, which would have disturbed the invalid: while Clara's second suggestion, that baby should have some pudding, appeared to give entire satisfaction, and produced perfect calm, under which state of things the visitors rose to go, Mabel not having exchanged a word either with mother or children the whole time, and standing on the threshold of the door, waiting for her cousin, who was shaking hands with Mrs. Simmons, and bestowing a parting kiss on the red round cheeks of the now smiling baby.

The young people walked on a short distance in silence; each had their own peculiar thoughts of the other. Mabel was the first to break calm. Then she said: 'How you could kiss that dirty little thing and offer to nurse it, I can't conceive, Clara; it quite sickens me to think of it,' said Mabel, with something like a shudder. 'I wonder Aunt Mary sends us to such places; it is work for Bridget to do, and not for us,' she continued. 'I don't think my mamma would approve of my going.'

'Oh, you are mistaken there, I know,' said Clara; 'for I have often heard aunt tell of the poor people your mamma and she used to visit, before Aunt Ada married—yes, and for a long time after she was married, until she was poorly, and then of course she was obliged to give up; but I'm quite sure she will be glad to hear of your doing the same. Now we must make haste, for fear we should be too late for dinner.'

# CHAPTER XV

## A CATASTROPHE

It was not a very pleasant trio that sat at the table the morning after the visit to the cottage. If Mabel had disliked the coarse work on which she had been employed the day before, her repugnance to the examination to which she was subjected by Aunt Mary, in order to test the capabilities of her niece, and to find out what lessons would be most appropriate for her, showed itself so plainly in fits of sullenness, or tears of vexation, that even Miss Livesay herself could not help feeling-dispirited; while Clara, though she tried to think only of her lessons, felt very much disposed to shed tears on her aunt's account. More than once, indeed, a subdued expression of rage escaped from the irritated Mabel; but it was so instantly and authoritatively checked by her aunt, that Mabel was made to feel that it would be useless for her to contend: so she sat and pored over her book in sullen silence.

This lasted until near dinner-time, so that the results of this morning's work, so far as Mabel was concerned, had been anything but satisfactory when the books were put away; and it was with very painful feelings that Miss Livesay contemplated not only the drudgery she would be subjected to, in having to go through *early lessons* with this refractory

Mrs. Perring

niece of hers (who was far, very far behind both Clara and the Maitlands in her learning), but the conflict she was likely to encounter with pride and obstinacy, evils she never before had to contend with.

Aunt Mary, however, was not one to give way to despondency, and at the dinner-table she had resumed all her usual cheerfulness; nor did she make the least difference in her manners to her nieces, but chatted with them both, as if nothing had occurred to disturb her serenity.

The mornings at Oak Villa were always devoted to lessons; in the afternoon there were two hours spent in work and reading; then the day's duties were finished, if we except the looking over the lessons for the following day, which Clara never omitted doing. And on this day she had a scheme in her head, both for doing Mabel good, and saving her dear aunt trouble.

In short, she determined, if possible, to induce her cousin to exert herself in learning extra lessons, in order to overtake the young Maitlands and herself.

She thought, perhaps, that the very pride in the young girl's composition would aid her in this task, and in this she was not mistaken. Mabel this afternoon was permitted to do some of the work she had brought from home; and what with this indulgence, and the clever and amusing book her aunt had been reading to them, she had quite recovered her spirits, and was as lively and cheerful as possible.

'Isn't it time to feed the fowls, Clara?' inquired Mabel, when work and books were laid aside.

'Yes, dear, it is,' replied her cousin; 'but I should be obliged if you would feed them for me to-day, as Aunt Mary wants me to write a letter to dear mamma before post-time.'

'Oh, I shall be glad to do so, very glad!' said Mabel, who had her own motives for the alacrity she displayed.

'Must I ask Bridget for the corn?' she inquired.

'I dare say you will find it set ready on the kitchen table; Bridget never forgets,' said Clara, as she arranged her desk and writing materials.

Mabel ran off in great glee, and was soon busily engaged in her very agreeable task; yet in spite of her endeavours, she found that it was impossible to give satisfaction to all her feathered friends. Some were too greedy, and would insist upon having more than their share, while others were not courageous enough to stand up for their rights, and so were easily repulsed, and came very badly off in the general scramble, notwithstanding Mabel's spirited attempts to make an equitable distribution. At last she got tired of trying to teach manners to the cock and hens, so she went to look after the pets, as she called the chickens. These, as we have before stated, had with their mother a separate establishment, and so they were permitted to peck their grains in peace, being in no danger of losing their share; though even among these tiny things there were contentions for a single grain, which perhaps three or four would strive after. As Mabel stood watching and admiring the little downy creatures, the desire came strongly over her, as it had done before, to take one up in her hand.

'What harm could I do the little creature by just holding it in my hand for a minute?' said Mabel. 'And as to the old hen pecking at me, I don't care for that; and I dare say,' she added, 'Clara only told me this to frighten me.'

As Mabel made this very unjust remark concerning her cousin, she opened the small door in the wire-work, and put her hand in to seize one of the chicks; but she was saluted with such a terribly hard peck from Dame Netty, that, had she not been very determined in the matter, she would have let the little chick go. Unfortunately for the little creature, her captor was very determined, and in spite of the hard peck, and the struggles of the bird, she took it out, and was in the act of shutting to the door, when the soft trembling thing slipped out of her hand, and fluttered away to its own destruction.

Yes, there on the wall, slyly watching all that had been going on, and with as great a desire after the chicken as Mabel herself had, though for a vastly different purpose, sat the fine sleek cat, to whom my young readers have before been introduced, and quick as lightning she pounced down upon the poor chick, and carried it off.

This was a terrible catastrophe, and Mabel stood for a moment in bitter dismay; she did not know what to do—how should she? The cat had disappeared, and by this time the poor chicken was killed, and perhaps eaten. Should she tell Clara? no, that would never do, for it would be sure to come to Aunt Mary's ears. It was not the first scrape that Mabel had got into, and we are sorry to add got out of by dissimulation; and now, after a little further consideration, she came to the unwise conclusion that it would be better to say nothing about the matter. After all, it was only one chick out of twelve; it perhaps would not be missed. And though she was sorry that the poor little thing had been killed, she solaced herself with the idea that there would soon be a fresh brood to attract her cousin's attention.

Comforting herself with this idea, she walked into the dining-room, where she found the tea ready, and was soon joined by her aunt and cousin, who had finished their correspondence, and were now at liberty to take their evening walk as soon as the pleasant meal was ended.

# CHAPTER XVI

## A VISIT TO THE VICARAGE

During tea-time, Aunt Mary proposed a walk to the vicarage, as she wanted to ask Mr. Newlove's opinion of the state of poor Simmons, as well as to inquire after the welfare of some of her pensioners, whom she had not yet had time to visit since her return home. The proposal pleased Clara, with whom the gentle Newlove was an especial favourite; though Mabel had conceived a dislike that she could give no reason for, to this quiet, sensible, and affectionate girl.

It was with very different feelings that the cousins went upstairs to dress. Mabel, we must suppose, thought that as she was going to a clergyman's house, she should have to listen to a sermon; or if not that, to sit still, and say nothing, while the seniors talked about sick folks, and old men and women, till she should be quite wearied out; and this was certainly no pleasant prospect for a lively young lady. But Mabel said nothing of all this; as usual, her conversation turned on what she should wear.

'Are you not going to change your dress, Clara?' said her cousin; 'you are surely not going to the vicarage in that dowdy-looking frock? Why, it is only fit to wear in the mornings, or to go visiting to dirty cottages, such as we went to yesterday.'

'Now don't let us talk about dress,' said Clara; 'my frock is what Aunt Mary bought for me, and if she thinks it good enough for me to wear, I'm sure I do too. Besides, Mabel, you are very much mistaken if you think that Mr. or Mrs. Newlove would notice your dress, unless, indeed, it were a very smart one, such as I know they wouldn't like.'

'Then I shan't care for *their* likes, but I shall just put on what *I like* myself,' said the graceless girl, as she took from her drawer a very pretty printed muslin, and proceeded to array herself in it, finishing off by donning a little black hat with a white feather in it.

'Now, suppose it should rain,' suggested Clara, 'what becomes of your pretty frock and your white feather?'

'There is not the least likelihood of rain,' replied Mabel; 'I never saw a finer evening;' and away she ran downstairs, but taking care to avoid a meeting with her aunt until they were all ready to start.

It was indeed a lovely evening for a walk. It had been very hot at one time of the day, but there had been a thunder-shower in the afternoon, which had cooled the air, and given freshness of colouring to the surrounding vegetation, deepening the tints on flower and shrub and tree, while,

'The ling'ring sun seem'd loth to leave  Landskip so fair, to gentle eve.'

Aunt Mary, though of course she noticed the difference in the dresses of her nieces, said nothing about it; but kept up, as she usually did, a conversation both amusing and instructive. Even Mabel forgot her fine clothes in listening to her aunt, and for the present seemed to be thrown out of self. Such a charm is there in wise teaching.

Nor when they reached the pretty, secluded vicarage, and were heartily welcomed by its inmates, were the fears of Mabel at all likely to be realised, as instead of having to listen to a sermon, or details of old and sick people, she and Clara were walked off by Robert and Edith Newlove, to see the rabbits, and the ringdoves, and the poultry in their respective habitations.

'How beautiful they are—how very beautiful!' said Clara, speaking of the ringdoves; 'and so gentle too—they don't fight and squabble like my hens do over a few grains of wheat.'

'Oh, they can peck one another sometimes,' said Edith; 'but they are not noisy about it like the fowls.'

'And my rabbits are not at all noisy either,' said Robert; 'but the buck can be very cruel, for if we don't take care he makes nothing of eating up one or two of the little ones.'

'Horrid creatures!' said Mabel. 'I shall never like rabbits again; it is quite shocking.'

'It would indeed be quite shocking if they knew better,' replied Robert; 'but they don't, so we must try to prevent them from acting cruelly. And after all,' he added, 'it is not half so bad as boys and girls doing wrong when they know better; yet we should not say of them that we should never like them again, should we, Miss Mabel?'

'No, I suppose not,' said the conscience stricken girl, as she found herself standing before the fowls' house, which was the very model of Clara's, and indeed had been made by the same industrious hands, namely those of poor Simmons, who was now, and had been for months, lying on the bed of languishing.

'You see the fowls are all gone to roost,' said Edith; 'the dear little chicks are under their mother's wing. I do wish you could have seen them; there are ten such beauties!'

'Oh, I have got twelve,' cried Clara; 'and in a few days' time I expect we shall have twelve more, if Dame Partlet is as fortunate as Netty. Do come and see them, Edith dear, next week. Think what a family I, or rather Aunt, will have to provide for—twenty-four!'

This was indeed not only counting the chickens before they were hatched, but not counting on misfortunes to those that were already hatched, and Mabel did not feel at all comfortable at the turn the conversation had taken; she was not sorry, therefore, when the servant came to say that Miss Livesay thought it time to go home.

Of course the summons was immediately obeyed, and with very kind adieus, the friends, old and young, separated; Aunt Mary observing that 'they must walk rather quicker in returning home than they had in coming, as there were some stormy-looking clouds hanging overhead.'

The mention of clouds and showers turned Mabel's attention to her dress, which, to say the truth, she had forgotten; and no wonder, as no one had taken the slightest notice of it, though the foolish girl had been at such trouble to make herself attractive. The mention of clouds and rain brought back Mabel's thoughts to the delicate frock and the new hat. She and Clara were a little in advance of their aunt, who had stopped for a moment to place a trifle in Mr. Newlove's hand for a very poor parishioner of his, of whom they had been talking.

'Oh, do let us run!' cried Mabel, as she looked up, and noticed the gathering clouds; 'perhaps we may get home before it begins to rain, if we make haste.'

'But Aunt Mary can't run,' replied Clara, 'and I am sure I shall not leave her; so you will have to run by yourself, Mabel, if you do go.'

'I'm not going to have my dress spoiled,' said the excited girl, as she gathered up her pretty skirt, and commenced to walk very rapidly at first; but as her fears increased from feeling, as she thought, a drop of rain, the rapid walking turned into a run, not quick enough, however, to bring her to the desired haven before the threatened shower descended, and, in spite of her exertion, seemed likely to drench her to the skin before she could arrive at Oak Villa. There had been trees in the way home, under which she might have found shelter if she had not been in such a violent hurry. Now it was too late for Mabel, though Clara and her aunt were actually at the time standing secure beneath the leafy screen; not certainly in a very comfortable state of mind, for Miss Livesay knew that her niece could not have reached home before the drenching shower descended, and she felt very uneasy on her account.

'I do hope that Bridget will take care that Mabel changes all her clothes,' said Aunt Mary; 'she must be wet through if she has been out in the rain. The showers are so very heavy, though they do not last long.'

'I think this shower is nearly over now; do you think we may venture to go, aunt?' inquired Clara, who partook of her aunt's anxiety respecting her cousin.

'Yes, dear; we have nothing on to spoil. A few drops will not do us any harm, and I fancy we shall have another downpour if we wait longer.'

This was Aunt Mary's decided opinion, and on the strength of it, the anxious pair set forward on their way home, which place they certainly would not have reached with dry clothing, had not careful Bridget suddenly made her appearance with cloaks and umbrellas.

This was rather an uncomfortable ending to a pleasant evening, but life has ever its ups and downs, its sunlight and its shadows, for the young as well as for the old. So it has ever been, and so it will ever be to the end of time.

It would have been well for Mabel Ellis if the spoiling of her dress had been the worst result of her foolish pride. And yet, perhaps, I ought not to say that it would not have been well had the trouble ended there. Adversity is a *very stern*, but a *very wise* teacher. We may not always see this to be so, and we may be very loth to acknowledge it, but it is a fact nevertheless. Aunt Mary's first thought, when she entered the house, was for Mabel, whom she found by the kitchen fire drying her petticoat, the muslin dress having been taken off, and hung over a chair.

'Have you changed shoes and stockings, my dear?' was the first question, which was answered in the negative. But we will leave further details for the next chapter.

# CHAPTER XVII

## A SERIOUS ILLNESS

As we have before stated, Mabel had only changed her upper garments. Stockings and shoes, though soaked through in coming along the wet grass, she had not thought of, and her wet petticoat steamed and smoked as she stood drying it by the kitchen fire.

'Dear me! dear me!' exclaimed Aunt Mary; 'why did you not immediately take off all your wet clothes? Clara dear, go with Mabel upstairs, help her to undress and get into bed, and I will bring some warm tea up as soon as possible. I am quite distressed to see the state you are in, my dear,' she added.

Mabel, though of course obliged to obey, went off very reluctantly, declaring all the time that she should be no worse for the wetting, and feeling far more concerned about the spoiling of her dress and her hat, than fearful of any consequence that might ensue from keeping on her wet clothes.

The room in which the cousins slept opened into one that was occupied by their aunt, so that she could easily communicate with them if anything was the matter. Strict in requiring obedience to her commands, and in not permitting any of her rules to be disregarded, Miss Livesay was still a most loving and unselfish relative and friend, untiring in the kind attentions to the sick, ever glad and ready to relieve the needy, or to give a word of advice or sympathy when it was likely to be well received. All the household had retired to rest but herself; she had seen her dear children, as she often called Clara and Mabel, fast asleep in their separate little white beds, but she still felt anxiety on Mabel's account.

'Poor, foolish girl,' said the kind aunt to herself, 'I wonder whether I shall ever be able to convince her of her folly. I cannot change her heart, but I will pray that it may be changed; and I will do everything in my power, both by example and precept, to show her that "Wisdom's ways are ways of pleasantness, and her paths peace."' As Miss Livesay said this, she once more went to look at the sleepers in the adjoining room. Clara lay pale, peaceful, and soundly asleep; but Mabel, though also asleep, looked flushed, and appeared restless.

This, Aunt Mary thought, might arise from the hurry and agitation of running home so quickly; she did not wish to meet evils half-way, yet, on retiring from the room, she made up her mind to take another look at the sleeping girl during the night. This she accordingly did, but observing no fresh symptoms for alarm, she lay down again, and only waked when Clara came to tell her that Mabel complained of great pains in her limbs. This sad news completely awed the kind aunt, for she dreaded an attack of rheumatic fever, as Mabel's mamma had been a dreadful sufferer two years before from that very serious malady. As soon as possible, the doctor was sent for. Aunt Mary was no alarmist, and could herself have dealt with any ordinary complaint; but she wished to have the doctor's opinion, and, if possible, his decision, on the real nature of the illness from which her niece was suffering, in order that she might act with befitting caution, if there were any likelihood of infection.

Clara sat disconsolate by the side of the pretty white bed, where her poor cousin lay with feverish head and aching limbs. The stricken girl was very quiet, except when she made an attempt to move, and then the pain caused her to utter a faint cry, which thrilled through Clara's kind heart; for she had never before been called upon to watch by a sick-bed.

'Oh, dear Mabel, I am so sorry for you,' said the affectionate child-nurse; 'I wish I could do anything to give you relief from your pains.'

'Thank you, dear Clara,' said the poor girl, in a quiet, subdued tone, very unlike that of the preceding day; even in this short time reflection had been at work, conscience had not been inactive, for retribution seemed to have come so suddenly as a necessary consequence of wrongdoing.

But the doctor is here now; we must not keep him waiting. A kind, fatherly, benevolent-looking man stands beside the bed of pain, on one side, and the loving, anxious aunt and cousin on the other.

'You are quite right in your idea as to the nature of the complaint, dear madam,' said Dr. Madox. 'Your niece is suffering from an attack of rheumatic fever; a very sharp attack it appears to be, but it need not on that account be a long one, though, just now, it is impossible to predict. However, we will do all we can for her,' added the doctor, cheerfully; 'in the meantime, you know, of course, that there is no danger of infection, though I should advise the patient to be kept perfectly quiet.'

This was indeed a very painful trial for all parties; but Aunt Mary felt that the hand that afflicts can also sustain. She knew, also, that pain and suffering and sorrow are often antidotes to the much more serious evils of pride and vanity and sinful tempers, and that, when they are submitted to patiently, they bring forth excellent fruits.

'Let me nurse dear Mabel myself, aunt,' said Clara; 'I will do everything I can do for her night and day. Oh, I do hope she will soon be well again!'

'And I *hope* so too, my dear Clara,' replied her aunt; 'but you must not think that you can attend to your cousin without help. You may of course remain with her for company; and this need not perhaps hinder your lessons, unless she should become very impatient, as is often the case with sufferers in this severe malady. But health, your health, my child, must be attended to; you must have air and exercise. And I fear that we shall all be required to lend a helping hand to the poor invalid should the fever greatly increase. I am just going to write to my sister, Mabel's mamma. I must be careful not to alarm her, in her weak state, as she is very nervous. You can return now to your cousin,' continued Aunt Mary, 'and be sure you do not leave her alone until I come to you. Ring for anything that is wanted.'

And now for weeks and weeks, this same selfish, self-willed girl, Mabel Ellis, lay on the bed of pain and languishing, and I may add, I am rejoiced to say, on the bed of sincere repentance. Yes, the salutary lessons of adversity had not been taught in vain, for they were not transitory ones, they had taken deep root; while the Divine precepts and heavenly counsels, which she had heard daily from her most loving and tender nurses, sank deep into a heart out of which had been weeded, to make room for them, the rank and bitter weeds of pride and passion.

Mabel Ellis was indeed an altered character, when able once more to sit up in the arm-chair; though so weak that she could scarcely speak above her breath, her looks of love and thankfulness, and the soft eyes often filled with glad tears, spoke most expressively to the hearts of her aunt and cousin, for they felt that their labour of love had not been in vain; and though all Aunt Mary's usual routine had been put aside, and for a time a new phase of life had been set before her, in this trial she could feel thankful.

'The seeds of affliction and pain,
When the soil has been moistened with rain
That flow'd from a penitent heart,
Into beauty, and fragrance will start.

'Oh flowers of celestial birth!
Though springing from clods of the earth,
How rich are the odours ye shed
O'er the couch where the languishing head

'Is pillow'd in gentle repose,
Forgetting awhile its past woes;
Then waking, the incense of praise,
With your odorous breathings, to raise.'

None but those who are recovering from a serious illness can conceive the feelings of gratitude and love which take possession of the heart when it is rightly disposed, what time the rod of affliction is removed. Mabel seemed to feel herself a new creature, and as she threw her arms round her cousin's neck, she gave expression to feelings of thankfulness and love for the kind attention she had received from her and from her aunt. She did not fail to lament bitterly the pride and sinful temper, which now appeared to her to have been the principal cause of all her trouble.

It was while she was thus bitterly lamenting the past, and weeping on Clara's shoulder, that Aunt Mary came rather suddenly into the room and surprised them.

'Come, my children,' said the kind lady, 'this will never do! Nurse and convalescent both in tears,' she added, for Clara was also weeping; 'I am afraid, dear Mabel, I shall have to dismiss your young attendant, and engage one with more judgment and with less sympathy.'

'Oh no, no, dear aunt,' was the ready response. '*I* will behave better, I assure you,' said Clara. 'Poor Mabel is weak, and a little thing makes her cry. She is only sorrowing now for the past; you will teach her, I know, to hope for the future.'

'Yes, even while we sorrow, we must hope; hope is the great lightener of all trouble. Come, cheer up, my child,' said Aunt Mary; 'I have some pleasant news for you to-day. I have just had a letter from Camden Terrace, to say that your papa and mamma and Freddy are coming to see you this afternoon, and to drink tea with me. Ah, I see you can smile, and be glad. We must have no more tears to-day; entertain only thoughts of love and thankfulness.'

# CHAPTER XVIII

## A FAMILY PARTY

What a blessing it is to be possessed of a happy and cheerful disposition!

And who so likely to have such blessing as those who not only *say* 'Our Father which art in Heaven,' but believing what they say, 'try to walk with Him in love, as dear children.' Such persons diffuse cheerfulness all around them; while on the contrary, those who are selfish and passionate, sow the seeds of trouble and discontent broadcast around them. And pride—oh, that hateful sin—what have children to do with pride? Helpless and dependent as they are on parents or friends, what have they to be proud of? Nothing!

Look at that curly-headed little boy, Freddy Ellis, who would be beautiful were it not for the disdainful curl on his upper lip, and the indignant expression in his eye when he has received some supposed affront. Listen to the passionate vehemence of his words when he is refused some indulgence which he has been teasing his mamma to grant him, though it would surely try your patience, as it has done mine, to hear the stamping and screaming that is going on just outside the parlour-door; and yet, for all this, Freddy receives no punishment. Oh no! 'It would break his spirit.' What absurd reasoning!

Do we inquire from whom is this spirit, which has more of the *serpent* than the *dove*? The answer will be, 'It is *not* from the meek and lowly Saviour!'

Oh parents, whoever you be, take care lest you foster the serpent that will diffuse its subtle poison over the cherished blossoms which you are, or *ought to be*, training for heaven, and leave a sting which may pierce your own hearts. One thing we may be sure of, that the faults which we, through negligence or weak indulgence, leave unchecked in our children in early life, a wiser though severer hand than ours will use the rod of correction to eradicate. And can this really be *love*, that puts off the proper time of chastisement, knowing that it is likely to be doubled on that account? Alas, no!

But I must crave pardon for sermonising, and return to the sick chamber, for Mabel's papa and mamma have come to pay their promised visit. Poor girl, she is so thin and pale that papa, who has only seen her twice during her illness, is quite shocked, and sitting down beside the arm-chair, declares that he can scarcely believe she is his once plump, rosy girl. Mamma has seen her often, and has shed many a tear over her suffering child; but still it was a comfort to her to know that Mabel was in such good hands. Sister Julia is also here, looking very sorrowful; but Aunt Mary says:

'Now I am not going to permit anybody who draws a long face to remain in my nursery; so those who look as if they were preparing to cry, instead of to smile, must please take a walk in the garden, till they have recovered themselves. What say you, Freddy, to this?' inquired Aunt Mary of her little nephew, who stood looking on, not knowing seemingly

　　　　　　　Mrs. Perring

whether he was expected to smile or to cry, though on hearing his aunt's cheery address, he came to the conclusion that it was not necessary for him to commence the disagreeable alternative, although it must be confessed he was a ready practitioner in yelling bouts.

'I should like to go into the garden, aunt,' responded Freddy. 'I want to see Clara's hens and chickens; may I go now?'

'No, not just now, dear,' replied his aunt; 'your cousin will go with you presently; she is engaged just at present, so you will have to wait.'

This waiting, however, did not at all suit the impatient spirit of Master Fred, and on Aunt Mary's going out of the room he gave expression to his vexation.

'Why can't I go into the garden by myself, I wonder?' he exclaimed passionately to his mamma, by whose chair he was standing. 'Aunt needn't think that I should hurt the fowls; it is very unkind of her.'

All this was said in a subdued tone, that papa, who was talking with Mabel, might not hear.

'Hush, hush, Freddy!' said his mother; 'your Aunt Mary is never unkind: you should not say such things of her.'

'But *I* think she is very unkind,' repeated the boy emphatically, as if what he said must settle the point; but it only drew the attention of his papa, who inquired what the vehement talking was about, and threatened severe punishment if any of Fred's tempers were exhibited at Oak Villa.

'Don't check the poor child so harshly,' said unwise mamma;

'he only wants his aunt to let him go and see the fowls. And really I think she might let him go, for he could do no harm.'

Mr. Ellis had a strong inclination to reply to this ill-advised speech, but he looked at the pale face beside him, and prudently forbore any further remark.

A nicely spread tea-table, on which there were plenty of cakes, smoothed down the ruffled temper of the spoilt boy; yet he did not forget what had all along been uppermost in his mind, namely, that he was to go and see the chickens as soon as tea was over. Had Mr. Ellis not been afraid of creating a disturbance at Oak Villa, he would certainly have prevented Fred's going into the garden, after his display of temper in his sister's room. He, however, made no opposition when the impatient boy, having despatched his tea and cake, made the announcement to his cousin Clara, that he was ready to go with her to see the fowls; and she good-naturedly rose from the table to attend him—not, however, without asking her aunt's leave.

Freddy of course was delighted with all he saw, though he said he thought the chickens were very large ones, and inquired after those he had seen a month ago, being very difficult to be persuaded that those he was now looking at were really the very identical chickens.

Like his sister Mabel, Freddy wanted to nurse one of the chickens; nor did he ask if he might do so, but while Clara went for the corn he opened the wire door and boldly thrust his hand in: only, however, to receive, as she had done, a severe peck from the hen, which sent him stamping and screaming up and down, no doubt to the great astonishment of the cock and hens, and the immediate disarrangement of the family party, who all rushed out to know what was the matter. It certainly was a severe peck that the old hen had given, and a very great fright that the household had been put into by the screams and the roaring of the cowardly boy, which continued as he clung to his mamma's dress, until he accidentally caught sight of his papa, and then the storm ceased as if by magic; and so much of sham had there been in the affair, that the tempest calmed down without leaving trace of sob or tear.

Mr. Ellis saw that his presence had been effectual, so he only said a few words to the young rebel, but he cast a half-sorrowful, half-angry glance at his wife; and Aunt Mary could not help whispering, 'Ada, what troubles you are making for yourself!'

# CHAPTER XIX

## MAY DAY

It was months before Mabel could really be said to have regained her health and strength. The dreary winter had passed away, and the tender leaves, and blossoms of April, had put forth their signs of returning spring.

It must not however be supposed that the cold and dark season had been an unprofitable one; far from it. Though Mabel had been an occasional sufferer, during all that time, she and Clara had diligently attended to their studies, and had, Aunt Mary said, made rapid advance; while the inward change which had been experienced by the invalid left no room for regret either to herself or her friends.

Mabel knew and felt that she had been healed of a far worse malady than any bodily one, and though, as in the case of rheumatic pains, hidden evils still gave occasional inward spasms, she had learned at whose hands she was to receive the healing draught, and she never failed to apply for it in the hour of need.

I ought perhaps to have informed my readers, that soon after Mabel had been taken ill, Mr. and Mrs. Maitland, with their two daughters, Dora and Annie, had gone to spend the winter months in the west of England, with that lady's mother, who was now far advanced in years, and very desirous of having the company of this her last surviving child, and to feel the cheering influence of lively girlhood in the society of her truly loving and attentive granddaughters.

And now, as I have before said, the winter had gone, and dewy April, with its smiles and tears, its soft green, tender leaves, its embryo buds and blossoms, its morning saluta-tions which blithe birds sang in the half-clothed trees or in the air, made fragrant by the breath of primrose pale, or violet blue, or polyanthus bright—yes, dewy April, notwith-standing all these delights, was about to take its departure, in order to make way for the pleasant month of May, whose praises Aunt Mary celebrated in rhyme. Oak Villa was indeed a highly privileged home; no young girl, whose mind was properly balanced, could have considered it otherwise. Its owner was cheerful as the lark, industrious as the bee, thoughtful and provident as the ant, benevolent as!—well, I won't liken her to any of our four-footed friends; indeed, just at this moment, I must confess that no comparison occurs to me: but Aunt Mary loved her nieces, delighted to impart to them those stores of knowledge to which she was herself constantly adding, and which a very retentive memory enabled her to draw on for almost any occasion.

Master Freddy, who, in his visit to the truly happy home I have been speaking of, had contrived to make himself as disagreeable as possible, had been punished for his conduct by being prevented from going with his sister Julia in her occasional visits to Oak Villa; this, of course, was by papa's order, and the prohibition was almost as grievous to mamma as it was to Freddy, but there was no redress. Julia had enjoyed many a pleasant walk with her sister and cousin, and she was particularly fond of going to see the poor people, especially Mrs. Simmons, whose husband had in a great measure regained his strength, and was now able to do at least some little towards the maintaining of his family. It had been very dull at home for Julia, after her sister had gone to Oak Villa; but she had her mamma to attend to, and to teach the children, though to say the truth this latter was almost an impossibility where Freddy was concerned, so he was often sent down to stay with mamma, being pronounced incorrigible.

But May morning has come at last; it is Aunt Mary's birthday, and such a lovely day! The cousins have a great deal of work to do before breakfast-time: may-blossoms to gather, garlands to twine, vases to fill with the sweet-scented early flowers, the breakfast-table to arrange with the best possible taste. As to Bridget, she had the day before been preparing for this special holiday; and even now she is very busy with her hot cakes and buns, which bid fair to be of the very best quality. Nine o'clock was the appointed hour for breakfast, and as Aunt Mary was not permitted by the young decorators to see what had been done in the way of preparation, it had been agreed that prayers were to be read in her bedroom, where, at half-past eight, Clara and Mabel, and Bridget, made their appearance; the former clasping Aunt Mary's neck, kissing her, and offering their most sincere and loving good wishes, the latter looking on the while, with no less kindly feeling, and with the honest tears of a faithful and devoted heart in her eyes.

Punctually at nine, a cab drove up to the garden-gate of Oak Villa, which Bridget stood ready to open, while Clara and Mabel waited at the hall-door, to receive the joyful little party, and Aunt Mary formed the background of the scene.

'How smart you are, Freddy,' remarked Clara, as she handed that young gentleman out of the cab; 'why, I never saw you in that dress before.'

'We were kept waiting some time,' said his mamma, 'because he would not have his other clothes on. I was afraid we should be too late, so I let him have his own way.'

'As usual, my dear sister,' said Aunt Mary, smiling, as she kissed and welcomed her sister. 'I'm afraid Freddy's light clothes will come to grief before the day is over, but he must take care.'

'Oh, how beautifully you have set out the table!' was the general exclamation as they all entered the breakfast-room together; and really, it was a very imposing sight, and the juveniles thought a very appetising sight, for ham, and eggs, and tongue, and chicken, and cakes, and buns, make a strong appeal for their share of commendation, even where the more delicate and refined tastes are attracted by beautiful colours and delicious odours.

It is really a very pleasant party that sits round this well-appointed table, though the kind and hospitable hostess regrets much that her brother-in-law, Mr. Ellis, was not able to be of the company. Aunt Mary knew who it was that kept order at home, and much, very much did she wish that her sister would be guided by her husband in the management of their children. But now there is nothing but bright looks and smiling happy faces, if we except that of Master Fred, who is looking round at the several dainties, apparently considering which he shall choose from first.

Unfortunately for the peace of society, Aunt Mary helped Freddy to some ham without being asked, and before that young gentleman had made up his mind as to what he should choose. This was indeed a sad mistake, though done without the slightest suspicion of giving offence; but the offence was very quickly manifested.

'I didn't want ham,' said the rude boy, as he pushed his plate from him; 'I wanted some tongue.'

'That is not a proper way to speak, my dear,' said his aunt; 'and you must eat what I have given you first, then you shall have some tongue.'

This was strange language to the wayward boy; he resented it by another push of his plate, and leaning back in his chair with the determination of a martyr.

Wonderful, he thought it, that no one at the breakfast-table, not even mamma, took the slightest notice of him, or seemed to care whether he had any breakfast or not. The fact was that a very significant look from Aunt Mary had imposed silence upon mamma, and sisters, and cousins, and the little ones were far too busy on their own account to give heed to Freddy, who was quarrelling with his bread and butter. In short, neither by word nor look had any effort been made to soothe the perturbed spirit of the really hungry boy.

This state of things, however, was not to be endured; so thought Fred, when, after waiting a considerable time, and casting furtive glances around to see if there were any signs in his favour, but perceiving none, he pushed his chair away from the table and rushed out of the room, quite unable longer to suppress his passion or his tears. This was the signal for Mrs. Ellis to remonstrate, which she had all along wished to do.

'Really, Mary, you are too severe on the poor boy,' she began, but was immediately, though kindly, silenced by Miss Livesay.

'Not now, if you please, dear,' said Aunt Mary; 'we will not discuss this point before the juveniles, we will talk it over by-and-by. In the meantime, Freddy has, I hear, gone into the garden, where he can amuse himself without getting into mischief.'

The latter part of this speech might have been omitted with propriety, but we must not forestall. The absence of the high-spirited young gentleman did not seem at all to lessen the enjoyment of the little people, who really behaved remarkably well, being for the most part under the management of a good nursery-maid, except when they were having their little lessons with Julia. Mrs. Ellis did not like the trouble of children herself, but through her weak-mindedness she certainly did what she could to make them a trouble to other people. The breakfast-party were just on the eve of breaking up, when a violent screaming in the back garden seemed to upset Aunt Mary's idea that Freddy could not get into any mischief there, and soon the whole party were in the back garden to ascertain the cause of the disturbance. There, at the large rain-water barrel, covered with wet and dirt, yet holding fast by the top, stood the unfortunate Fred, his face crimson with fear and excitement, while he still tried with all his might to turn back the tap which he had so unluckily loosened, and which now, like himself, refused to submit to a weak hand, but was readily reduced to order by a strong one; for Bridget was at the scene of action, and set free the boy, now completely shamed, if not subdued, by having to appear before the whole party as an object of commiseration, if not ridicule.

Of course there were no boy's habiliments at Oak Villa, and Fred had to undergo the further humiliation of being put into his sister's bed in one of her nightdresses, while his own clothes were drying.

It must be confessed that a great reaction had taken place since the cold water had been thrown on the fiery young spirit, for there had been more than the mere wetting of the body. Fasting also had done its beneficial work; the craving stomach seemed to be resisting the defiant will. And when Freddy found himself quietly between the sheets, with only his sister Mabel—who had brought some breakfast up—to witness his humiliation, he very gladly, I might almost say thankfully, turned *to* the tempting viands which he had so short a time ago turned *from* with disgust. Yes, the piece of ham was there, and this time it was not pushed back; but there was no tongue, which had been desired and denied before. Aunt Mary never did things by halves.

Here we will leave this graceless Freddy; he will have no lack of amusement while his clothes are drying, for Mabel and Clara have brought him books and pictures, and some old toys which had been put by: but Aunt Mary insists that Freddy is to be left to himself, after she has seen him, and kindly, but forcibly, shown him the foolishness, as well as the wickedness, of indulging in pride and evil temper. After all, May Day was at Oak Villa a very happy day to all who were there.

# CHAPTER XX

## AN EXCHANGE

Though the cold-water system had acted as a sedative with Master Fred, during the afternoon and evening of May Day, and though every precaution had been used to prevent any serious effects afterwards from the wetting, yet the boy did take cold; and so feverish and restless did he become, that the good Dr. Maddox, who had attended Mabel, was sent for without delay. His prescription, however, was not a very alarming one: namely, castor oil and some spirits of sweet nitre.

'Don't frighten yourself, dear madam,' said the doctor: '*this* is not a case of rheumatic fever; nothing but a slight influenza cold. But you must take care to give him the medicine.' The doctor laid great stress on this.

Of course the medicine was procured, but, alas! papa was not at home, and no amount of persuasion or coaxing would induce the obstinate little fellow to take it. It was in vain that mamma promised all sorts of toys, and produced preserves and lumps of sugar to take the taste out of his mouth, or threatened him with severe illness and more nauseous stuff, if this were not taken. It was no use, poor Mrs. Ellis was obliged to give it up; and heartily did she wish that her good sister Mary would call in the course of the day, for she dreaded her husband's coming home, and finding that the doctor's advice had not been followed. It was about three o'clock in the afternoon when the anxiously-expected visitor arrived at Camden Terrace. Of course she knew nothing about Fred being poorly; she had merely come to make general inquiries, and to see that Mrs. Ellis was no worse for the fatigue of May Day.

'Oh, I am better than usual, dear Mary,' she replied to the kind inquiry; 'but I am troubled about Fred now. He is very poorly, in bed, and the doctor has ordered medicine for him, which I cannot get him to take. I have been longing for you to come; will you try if you can induce him to take it?'

Aunt Mary smiled, as she said: 'Do you remember, dear, a former trial that I had with this young tyrant of yours, when, being very determined myself, I held him fast and pressed the glass to his mouth, whereupon he actually bit a great piece out of it, at the same time kicking me so violently that I was fain to let him go, with, I believe, a mental promise that I would never again subject myself to such an indignity?'

Mrs. Ellis could not help laughing; she had not forgotten the circumstance, but she pleaded now that Fred was two years older, and was not likely to repeat his exploit.

'I know he is two years older,' said Aunt Mary, 'but I don't feel at all certain that he is two years better than he was; though he may be so much stronger as to increase my difficulty.'

'Oh, do try, Mary dear,' urged Mrs. Ellis; 'I must get him to take it before his papa comes home.'

'Oh, Ada, Ada!' exclaimed her sister, 'how is it that you have allowed this boy to gain the mastery over you, to your own great sorrow, and to his great disadvantage? But, come,' added the kind friend, 'give me the medicine, and I will try what I can do.'

'Now, Freddy,' said his aunt, as she came into the bedroom, cup in hand, 'I am come to see you, and to make you better if I can. I suppose you are not fond of lying in bed this fine day,' she added.

'Oh no, aunt; I want to get up, but mamma won't let me.'

'Well, dear, you know, you must always try to do as mamma wishes you, because she knows what is best for you; but I have brought something from the doctor that is sure to do you good, and it is to be taken immediately.'

'I can't take it, aunt, it is such nasty stuff,' said the boy, with disgust.

'I know it is very nasty stuff, Freddy, and, like you, I can't bear to take medicine; but when I know that it is to make me well, I am not so foolish as to refuse it. So now sit up like a man, and take the cup in one hand, and this little mint-drop in the other; drink off the nasty stuff in a moment, and pop the mint-drop into your mouth at once; you will never feel the taste of the medicine after that.'

Whether it was the decisive manner in which Aunt Mary spoke, or the belief in the efficacy of the mint-drop, or the appeal to the manliness of the patient, we cannot say, but a magical effect had been produced, for the contents of the cup had been swallowed; and Fred, greatly relieved in mind, if not yet in body, laid down his head on the pillow and listened, evidently with much pleasure, to his aunt's commendations.

This short illness of Freddy's was followed by a much more serious one of his mamma's. It had been a long time coming on, and it was the doctor's opinion that it might be of some months' continuance; rest and quiet were ordered, but they are not easily obtained where there are refractory children at Freddy's age. It would be easy enough to keep the little ones quiet, but Mrs. Ellis had permitted this turbulent boy of hers to make appeals to her on every trifling occasion, and to stand and whine and cry until he obtained what he wanted, because mamma was worn out with his teasing. Now that she was really so ill as to be more than usually affected by any disturbance, it became a question with Aunt Mary (though it was to her a very painful one) whether it would not be expedient, and the right thing to do, to make an exchange in favour of the invalid, and to substitute Mabel for her brother Fred, taking the responsibility of that rather notorious rebel upon herself, and giving her dear sister the benefit of a tender nurse, who had grown wise beyond her years, through much suffering and good teaching.

If there had been the shadow of a doubt on the kind lady's mind as to what course she should pursue, her visit to Camden Terrace the day after the doctor had given his opinion respecting Mrs. Ellis, would have determined her; for on the front-door being opened, she heard a violent screaming and kicking, sufficient to disturb the nerves of a much less sensitive person than Mrs. Ellis.

'Oh, that is Fred making that noise,' said Mabel, who had come with her aunt to visit mamma. 'Shall I go up to him?' she inquired.

'No, my dear; go to the sick-room. I will myself encounter the rebel;' and Aunt Mary went straight upstairs, just as nurse opened the room-door to remonstrate with the unruly boy, who was quickly and unceremoniously caught up from the floor, and made to stand on his feet.

'Let me not hear another sound from you while I am here,' said his aunt. 'And, Jane,' she added, speaking to the nurse, 'please to put up in a small basket this young gentleman's night-clothes. I intend to take him home with me; he must not remain here to make his poor mamma worse than she is.' So saying, Miss Livesay left the nursery, and proceeded to her sister's bedroom, where she found Mabel arranging the pillows, and making the bed rather more comfortable for her poor mamma.

Master Freddy had been completely taken by surprise, and he seemed at a loss at first how to give vent to the suppressed passion that was swelling within; but when nurse said, 'I am very glad indeed that your aunt is going to take you away, for then we shall have some peace in the house,' he jumped off the stool on which he had been sitting, and would have struck her with a brush which he took from the table, had she not forcibly held both his hands, and threatened to take him at once to the room where Aunt Mary was.

'You needn't put up my night-shirt,' said passionate Fred, 'for I shan't go with that nasty old thing!' This was, however, uttered in a subdued tone, and elicited 'Shame, shame!' from nurse, and even from little Gerty.

'I think,' added Jane, 'you are the very worst boy I ever did see, and I wouldn't stop here if you was obliged to be kept in the nursery, which I suppose you would be, now your mamma's so poorly, for it isn't to be expected that you will be allowed to go teasing her about every little thing. I *am* glad, very glad, you are going away; and I hope Miss Livesay will keep you a very long time,' added nurse, while Fred, not daring to explode, on account of his aunt's being so near, vented his passion on the poor kitten by kicking it violently from under the stool, where he had again seated himself.

'Ada dear,' said Aunt Mary to her sister, 'I am going to propose a transfer, which, though I must confess it will be a very painful one to me, yet perhaps may in the end be good for all parties; and, I think, will prove for your especial benefit now you are so unwell. It is my intention—if you do not object,' continued Miss Livesay, 'to leave dear Mabel with you, and to take that refractory young gentleman, whose kicking and shouting, as I came to the door, must have disturbed you, home with me to Oak Villa. I intend to remain with you this afternoon, while Mabel goes to our house to tell Bridget to prepare a bed for Fred. I dare say, before I want to leave, Mr. Ellis will be home, and then I shall have no fear of a scene with Master Freddy: he will not venture on opposition when his papa is here.'

'Oh, dear Mary!' said Mrs. Ellis, 'how kind it is of you to care for me and mine so much! I can never thank you enough for what you have done for dear Mabel; but she, poor girl, won't like to stay in a sick-room.'

'Mamma dear, don't say that!' exclaimed the now affectionate Mabel; 'I will nurse you day and night. I shall only be doing for you what dear aunt and Clara did for me, when I was so ill.'

'Well now, you must give me some work to do,' said Aunt Mary; 'I will sit with your mamma while you go down and tell Bridget to prepare a bed in my dressing-room for your brother. I shall take care to keep him near me day and night.' This speech was addressed to Mabel, who was very glad to find that it was her aunt's intention to remain till the evening; she soon set off on her errand, though she feared she should be the bearer of no very pleasant news to Bridget, who

Mrs. Perring

would certainly not at all like the advent of such an unruly boy at their peaceful home.

'I'm sure our mistress will not let him have the lamp lighted in his bedroom all night, as nurse says he has at home,' said Bridget; 'so most likely that will be the first row he will make.'

'Oh, leave aunt to settle all that, Bridget,' said Mabel; 'you know how well she manages these matters.'

"Deed I do, Miss Mabel; and who knows,' said the honest, plain-spoken servant, 'but what she may make as great a change in Fred as she did in you!'

Bridget did not take into account the severe illness and mental suffering that had helped, with Aunt Mary's wise efforts, to work this reformation. She attributed all to her kind mistress. While Bridget attended to the commands of her mistress, Mabel went into the garden to gather some flowers for her mamma, as her aunt had requested her; and after bidding good-morning to the faithful servant, she wended her way quickly to her early home, thinking, as she went, what a blessing it was to have so kind a friend as Aunt Mary. During the time that Mrs. Ellis had been so unwell, the children had all dined together in the nursery at two o'clock; and Aunt Mary insisted that there should be no departure from this rule on her account, as she intended to make one of the party. At the hour appointed, the bell rang for dinner, and soon all were seated at the table but Fred; that young gentleman had chosen to make himself scarce, and notwithstanding the ringing of the bell, out of doors and in, a second time, he did not make his appearance.

Great was the consternation of nurse at not being able to find Freddy; she began to fear that he had run away from home to avoid going to Oak Villa. He had once played such a trick, and made everybody miserable until he was found in the evening, and brought home by a woman who washed for his mamma. Mabel and Julia did not feel at all comfortable, though Aunt Mary would not let them leave the table to go in search of the truant.

'Don't distress yourselves, my dears,' said Miss Livesay; 'depend upon it, the culprit is not very far off. Nurse and cook will look after him.'

And so the dinner proceeded, though Mabel would much rather have gone without, had she been permitted. All at once a thought struck her, and she exclaimed: 'I'll tell you where I think he is, aunt; where we once found him before!' and Mabel rose up and went to the window which looked on the side of the house where there was a large dog-kennel, and over it a wooden shed with a window in it, to which shed access was gained by a ladder. 'Yes!' exclaimed Mabel, 'I see the key is in the door where the apples are kept. We once found Fred there asleep on the straw; perhaps he is there now!' and the anxious girl was making her way out of the room, when a loud scream brought her back to the window, from which she beheld Freddy with his foot caught in the top step of the ladder, and his head ignominiously resting on the hard step.

Mabel was off in an instant, but quick as she was, cook was there before her, and Fred had been turned right side upwards, and his blubbered face wiped with that towel of all work, Susan's apron; while his forehead presented a lump sufficiently large to account for the explosion they had been treated to.

No doubt it had been Master Freddy's intentions, when he went into this hiding-place, to remain there all day, until

Mrs. Perring

Aunt Mary should take her leave; he did not know of her intention to remain at Camden Terrace until his papa came home, or perhaps he might have hit upon some other expedient. His idea was, that they would all be so frightened at having lost him, that when he did make his appearance, he would be received joyfully.

Whether it was that the sound of the dinner-bell had created a sensation of hunger not to be resisted, or the savoury smell of the nicely cooked viands had stimulated the stomach to rebellion, we cannot say; but Freddy roused himself from his recumbent position, and, as we have seen, came (very unintentionally) head foremost down the steps. Alas, there is no one to sympathise with him in his self-made trouble, Aunt Mary won't permit it; and Master Frederick Ellis has to dine in the kitchen, a most humiliating necessity which would not have been submitted to, but for the inward cravings which would not be resisted.

It was with the greatest satisfaction that Mr. Ellis, when he came home, heard of the kind proposal of his sister-in-law to take Freddy home with her; he said that he could never sufficiently thank her for the good she had done to Mabel, but he feared that Freddy would prove a more troublesome inmate to Oak Villa than ever she had been. Aunt Mary declared, however, to the great astonishment of Freddy, who was in the room at the time, that Oak Villa would not hold naughty people, whether they were men, women, or children; and that as soon as Fred had slept there one night, he would find himself quite another boy, and be ready to do anything that he was desired. Fred heard all this with 'wonder-working eyes;' we don't know whether he really believed it. But as he trudged silently along by his aunt's side, with the little basket in one hand, and her hand clasping his other, he thought what a strange place Oak Villa must be to make people good, whether they liked it or not.

Mr. Ellis wished very much to accompany his sister home, but she would not permit this.

'How can you think that I want a protector when I have Fred with me, papa?' she inquired. 'I know very well,' she added, 'that we shall soon be the best friends in the world; and Freddy will take all the trouble off my hands of feeding cousin Clara's chickens while she is away.'

I should have stated that Clara had gone on a short visit to her mamma.

The reference to the chickens was an excellent stroke of policy of aunt's; she felt the small hand, which she held, tighten in hers, and an inward feeling of satisfaction came over her spirit, as she said within herself, 'Love is a constraining power.'

# CHAPTER XXI

## THE NEW INMATE OF OAK VILLA

And now a new sort of life began, both at Oak Villa, and at Camden Terrace.

Mabel had promised her aunt (and she meant faithfully to fulfil that promise) to give what portion of the time she could spare from her attendance on mamma, to the lessons of her sister Julia, who was now far behind Mabel, and sadly needed a preceptress.

Well and amicably the two girls worked together; though there were trials of temper at times, when Julia did not seem to make such progress as her youthful instructress had anticipated. This, however, was only a trifling matter; there was peace in the house, and papa came home, not to be burdened with complaints, by domestic irregularities, but to be solaced by the loving attentions of his two girls, and amused by the sententious sayings of little prudish Gertrude, or the high spirits and happy gleefulness of Willie.

It was also a source of great comfort to him to know that Fred was in such good keeping; he could not doubt this, when he had practical proof before him daily, in the change that had been wrought in his eldest daughter. But how do they get on at Oak Villa, I wonder?

Admirably, I must say, considering that this is Aunt Mary's first attempt at taming an embryo lord of the creation. Is she very severe? By no means! Fred finds, to his great surprise, that 'this nasty old thing' works by love! and he is positively so full of employment and enjoyment, that he has no time to think of himself or to give way to evil temper. It must be owned (for there was no miracle in the case) that kind Aunt Mary had determined to give up this week, while Clara was away, to the instruction, amusement, and management of the Camden Terrace rebel; and though no outward sign betrayed the good lady's inward trials, it really was a week of trial to her. But she had succeeded to a wonder, so far as outward appearance testified, and worthy Bridget, who, by her good-nature helped on the reformation, declared herself astonished to find Master Freddy such a different boy to what she expected.

And so the weeks passed by. Fred still lived on at Oak Villa, a happy and a loving inmate. Clara had come home, and contributed not a little to Fred's enjoyment; they went out together to see all the poor people, and particularly the Simmons family, who were getting on very well, now that the father was recovered. Fred had a wheelbarrow and a nice box that Simmons had made him, and Clara and he worked away famously in the garden, weeding, or planting, or picking up stones. Aunt Mary says, 'This is what we have been trying to do for you, dear Freddy. Weeding out the naughty bitter weeds, putting in seeds that we hope will spring up, and grow to be beautiful flowers, and picking up the stones, that the soil may look smooth, and show that it is well taken care of.'

We must not forget the visits paid to dear mamma, twice a week, when that good lady was moved, even to tears, to see the great change, both in appearance and manner, that had taken place in her beloved child. She was much better, and the doctor thought that change of air would be the very best thing to restore her to health; but there were many things to be considered in the carrying out of such a proposal. Time may do wonders, but that time had not yet come; and we have travelled on a little too fast, I think, so we will go back to the first morning of Master Freddy's advent at Oak Villa. The first bell had rung, but Bridget was not satisfied to let the little boy's getting up depend on that, so she went and knocked at his door, and then peeped in.

'Why, bless me, Master Fred, are you not up yet?' exclaimed the good woman in pretended surprise. 'Why, the sun has been up a long time, and the birds are a-singing; and the fowls I know are wanting their breakfast, so I hope you will not keep them waiting very long. You must wash yourself well, and dress yourself nicely, and brush your hair, for I know your aunt can't abide to see slovenly children.'

After these instructions, Bridget made her exit; and Fred, the tiresome Fred, who when at home would only get up when he thought proper, jumped out of bed, put on his socks and shoes, performed his ablutions, and finished his dressing in a most satisfactory manner. Then he went down, and joined his aunt in the breakfast-room.

'Well, my dear Fred,' said the kind lady, taking her nephew by the hand and kissing him, 'I hope you are no worse for your fall yesterday, and that you have had a good night's rest?'

'Oh, I slept so well, aunt. It is such a nice little bed, I like it so much!'

'And have you, my child,' said his aunt, 'thanked the good

God who gave you sleep, and rest, and kind friends?'

'I haven't said my prayers, aunt,' replied Freddy; 'I don't always say them.'

'But you always wish to have kind friends, and a nice bed, and peaceful sleep, don't you, dear Fred?' said Aunt Mary.

'Yes, aunt, I do,' replied the boy.

'And don't you think you ought to be thankful when you have them?' was the next question.

Freddy hung down his head, but he whispered 'Yes.'

'Well, go then, my dear, and thank your heavenly Father for His goodness, and ask Him to bless you, and keep you from all evil to-day.'

And Freddy went back to his room, and knelt beside his little bed, and repeated the same prayer that he had said so many times before, without thinking even of what he was saying; but this time he did think.

After breakfast Fred went to feed the fowls, though this ought to have been done before; but this was a beginning, so it did not much matter. At ten o'clock he was called to his books, and Aunt Mary expected a trial, for Freddy had never been at school, and his teaching at home had been only such as he chose to receive from his mamma or his sisters, when he happened to be in the humour. Yet he was naturally a quick child, and but for temper, his aunt did not at all contemplate any difficulty; indeed, she had no reason to do so, with her method of teaching. She was never harsh, but she was strict in discipline. She knew, that to make children happy, it was not at all necessary that they should have their own way, though she never contradicted them without occasion. She, in short, treated them as reasonable creatures, as loving creatures, who required love to draw them out; and she had seen, and felt, the happy results of this treatment. After the first week there was no more trouble about lessons; and with the assistance of Bridget and Clara, who were both now really fond of the boy, and did many little things to contribute to his pleasure, Aunt Mary found that she need no longer have any dread of having taken into her happy domicile an inmate, who would destroy its hitherto peaceful character; and Fred never once expressed a wish to go and live at home again.

# CHAPTER XXII

## THE OAK AND THE LAUREL UNITED

More than four months had elapsed since Mabel had left Oak Villa to attend to her mamma, and Freddy had found a happy and delightful home in that very desirable locality. The days were shortening now, and the splendid autumn sunsets threw their gorgeous colouring over the trees, that had already put on their russet mantles, as if in anticipation of some great change. In human affairs it often happens that great changes come very unexpectedly, and so it occurred in the families with whom we have been the most familiar.

It was the beginning of October, when Aunt Mary received a letter from her friend Mrs. Maitland which greatly surprised, and at first grieved her not a little. It contained the startling intelligence that Mr. Maitland wished to let their pretty homes, the Laurels, as the very precarious state of health Mrs. Maitland's mother was in, rendered it absolutely necessary that they should remain with her for perhaps a very long time.

'Oh, Clara dear,' said her aunt, 'is not this sad news for us? I can scarcely believe it. Mrs. Maitland says they are not coming back; but are going to let the Laurels.

'How we shall miss them all, I fear we shall never get such good neighbours again,' said the lady, in a much more dolorous tone than was usual with her.

'Oh, I am so sorry!' exclaimed Clara, 'and so will Mabel be I know, for Dora and Annie were our very best friends. But who is that other letter from?' inquired the niece; 'I hope that does not contain bad news, aunt!'

Miss Livesay took up the letter spoken of; she had been so taken by surprise with the information contained in the first letter, that she had almost forgotten the other, which she now opened, and a glad exclamation which she uttered on reading the first line convinced Clara that there was salve for the wound which had been inflicted.

She was not kept in a state of suspense, the letter was from Irene (Mrs. Gordon), and the first line was: 'We are coming home to you, dear Mary!'

'Oh, when, aunt, when?' cried Clara.

'Wait, my dear, and you shall hear all,' replied Miss Livesay. '"Captain Gordon has got leave of absence for six months; will you, can you, dear Mary, let me come again to the dear old home? there is no place like it!" Dear Irene,' cried Aunt Mary, she little thinks how I long to see her, and the quick tears testified the melting heart.

Freddy all this time had stood an amazed listener; he could not at all make it out why the breakfast should be delayed, but he remembered Aunt Irene, and Captain Gordon, too, and he could somewhat enter into the pleasure manifested at the idea of their coming to see them, only he wished, notwithstanding, that Aunt Mary would pour the tea out, and allow him to begin his breakfast. This was done almost mechanically by Aunt Mary, her mind was already so full of projects, which, however, must be explained some time hence.

'Now the first thing we do, dear Clara, after breakfast,' said the kind aunt, 'must be to go to Camden Terrace; I hope your uncle will not have gone out, as I have a message for him from Mr. Maitland.'

'Oh then, do let Freddy and me go at once,' entreated Clara; 'we can be so quick, and we can tell Uncle Ellis that you are coming immediately, so that you need not hurry yourself, dear aunt.'

'Not a bad proposition, my little girl,' said her aunt; 'and Freddy, is he ready to go?'

'Oh yes, I am quite ready, and we can run all the way, and we can tell mamma that Aunt Irene is coming to see her; won't she be pleased? and so will Mabel and Julia. Oh, I am so glad, and Fred gave a remarkable caper, which not only threw himself down, but *overthrew* the gravity of both aunt and cousin, who laughed heartily at the grotesque way in which he exhibited his joy.

'We won't say anything about Aunt Irene's letter till you come,' whispered Clara to her aunt, but that lady said:

'Depend upon it, dear Clara, your mamma has got a letter, as well as myself, so this will be no news to her, though the Maitlands' communications will, and of this you need not say anything.'

Mr. Ellis was just preparing to leave home when Clara and Fred made their appearance.

'Why, you are early visitors this morning,' said that gentle-man, kissing, and shaking hands with the fresh, healthy looking messengers, and adding; 'has the postman's news made you run off in such a hurry?'

'Yes, it is the postman's news, uncle, that sent us here so soon,' said Clara, 'because Aunt Mary wants to see, and talk with you, before you go out; she will be here in less than half an hour, if you will kindly wait.'

'That I will do with pleasure, my little girl, and you and Fred can go and find out mamma, and Mabel, and Julia, and Gertrude, and Willie, for I can hear them all making a noise; this news about Aunt Irene has caused a great commotion in the house,' said Mr. Ellis.

Away ran Clara and Freddy, to find, as papa had said, a glad and rather noisy company in mamma's room. The invalid herself seeming evidently better for this piece of joyous excitement.

We may well believe that the noise was not lessened in the room by the advent of Clara and Freddy; the latter having, since his departure from home, and the good accounts received of him from Aunt Mary, become somewhat of a hero in the estimation of the little people and even of his sisters. But here are other visitors, Aunt Mary and Mr. Ellis appear upon the scene, and they both stand for a moment in silent astonishment at the uproar that is made.

'Well,' said Aunt Mary, after a moment's pause, 'this is not much like the chamber of an invalid; and yet you look wonderfully bright, my dear Ada,' she said to her sister, putting her arms round and kissing Mrs. Ellis, who was already up, and seated in her arm-chair.

'Oh, I am so much better, dear Mary; Irene's letter has acted like a cordial to me this morning; of course *you* have received one from her?' said Mrs. Ellis.

'Yes; and I have also had one from our friend Mrs. Maitland, which, as it requires advice and consideration, will also require a little peace and quietness, so we had better dismiss the joyous young party; they can finish off, and talk over pleasant affairs, in the nursery. What do you say to this, my dears?' inquired Aunt Mary.

'We all say yes, yes, aunt!' replied Mabel, catching up Willie, and making a speedy exit, followed by the whole troop of rejoicing spirits, who were not at all sorry to leave grave discussions to their seniors.

'And now,' said Miss Livesay, after the young tribe had left the room, 'let us proceed to business. I have had a letter this morning from our friends the Maitlands, and in it, a request from Mr. Maitland to you, dear brother, to help him in the letting of his house, as they do not intend to return.'

'Oh, how I wish we could take the Laurels, Arthur!' said Mrs. Ellis, eagerly; 'it would be so delightful to be near dear Mary; the thought almost makes me well, I declare,' she continued, as the colour mounted to her pale cheeks.

'It was the very idea that entered my head when I read the letter,' said Miss Livesay. 'I do think, dear Ada, that such a change of air and scene would be very beneficial to you; but, of course, it will require consideration, which, I know, your husband will give it.'

'I don't think that we should find any difficulty in letting *this* house,' observed Mr. Ellis; 'and I assure you, I am as anxious for a change as my wife is; though the distance from my office will be greater, I should not mind that; I think we should all be greatly benefited in health. I will myself write to Mr. Maitland this very day, and run the risk of letting our own house, rather than lose such a golden opportunity.'

My young readers, I dare say, know nothing about the troubles of a removal; I do, and I am not at all disposed to inflict details on them. All I have to say on the subject is, that matters were so speedily and amicably arranged, that the Laurels or Laurel Villa, received its new occupants before the month of November had commenced, and that so great an improvement had taken place in the health of Mrs. Ellis, as made the doctor, aye, and Aunt Mary too, suspect that the *nerves* had received a great deal too much consideration, and that henceforth they were not to claim more than their due share. We may imagine how busy Mabel, and Clara, and Julia, and even Freddy had been; and, oh! what a comfort it was to all parties, that now, neither Laurel Villa, nor Oak Villa, would receive ill-conditioned men, women, or children, for did not the kind and benevolent fairy preside over both houses?

Yes, she did; and I am bound to say that there was no opposition, for Aunt Mary's ways and doings had worked such wonders as disinterested love alone *can* work, and her heart was filled with joy and thankfulness at the success achieved.

Captain Gordon and Aunt Irene did not arrive in England so soon as had been expected, but they put in an appearance before Christmas, and were quite delighted with the change that had been made; and, oh! what a joyous party helped to make the splendid wreath for the decoration of Mr. Norton's church, at Christmas time; plenty of laurels, we know, they had close at hand, so that though there were other kind workers in this delightful employ, I think we may say that none excelled in design or quantity the productions of the two villas.

Our former friend, Harry Maitland, was on a visit to Mr. Newlove, and not a day passed during the Christmas week in which there was not an interchange of visits with the young people; and when on Christmas Day they all assembled at church, I don't think there could have been in England a happier or more thankful family party than that which came from the intertwined *Oak and Laurel*!

'*Order* is Heaven's first law!'

But *Love* is the elastic, all-embracing band, which, wreathed with amaranthine flowers, endures when time shall be no more!


THE END


Mrs. Perring

# Choose from Thousands of 1stWorldLibrary Classics By

A. M. Barnard
Ada Leverson
Adolphus William Ward
Aesop
Agatha Christie
Alexander Aaronsohn
Alexander Kielland
Alexandre Dumas
Alfred Gatty
Alfred Ollivant
Alice Duer Miller
Alice Turner Curtis
Alice Dunbar
Allen Chapman
Alleyne Ireland
Ambrose Bierce
Amelia E. Barr
Amory H. Bradford
Andrew Lang
Andrew McFarland Davis
Andy Adams
Angela Brazil
Anna Alice Chapin
Anna Sewell
Annie Besant
Annie Hamilton Donnell
Annie Payson Call
Annie Roe Carr
Annonaymous
Anton Chekhov
Archibald Lee Fletcher
Arnold Bennett
Arthur C. Benson
Arthur Conan Doyle
Arthur M. Winfield
Arthur Ransome
Arthur Schnitzler
Arthur Train
Atticus
B.H. Baden-Powell
B. M. Bower
B. C. Chatterjee
Baroness Emmuska Orczy
Baroness Orczy
Basil King
Bayard Taylor
Ben Macomber
Bertha Muzzy Bower
Bjornstjerne Bjornson

Booth Tarkington
Boyd Cable
Bram Stoker
C. Collodi
C. E. Orr
C. M. Ingleby
Carolyn Wells
Catherine Parr Traill
Charles A. Eastman
Charles Amory Beach
Charles Dickens
Charles Dudley Warner
Charles Farrar Browne
Charles Ives
Charles Kingsley
Charles Klein
Charles Hanson Towne
Charles Lathrop Pack
Charles Romyn Dake
Charles Whibley
Charles Willing Beale
Charlotte M. Braeme
Charlotte M. Yonge
Charlotte Perkins Stetson
Clair W. Hayes
Clarence Day Jr.
Clarence E. Mulford
Clemence Housman
Confucius
Coningsby Dawson
Cornelis DeWitt Wilcox
Cyril Burleigh
D. H. Lawrence
Daniel Defoe
David Garnett
Dinah Craik
Don Carlos Janes
Donald Keyhoe
Dorothy Kilner
Dougan Clark
Douglas Fairbanks
E. Nesbit
E. P. Roe
E. Phillips Oppenheim
E. S. Brooks
Earl Barnes
Edgar Rice Burroughs
Edith Van Dyne
Edith Wharton

Edward Everett Hale
Edward J. O'Biren
Edward S. Ellis
Edwin L. Arnold
Eleanor Atkins
Eleanor Hallowell Abbott
Eliot Gregory
Elizabeth Gaskell
Elizabeth McCracken
Elizabeth Von Arnim
Ellem Key
Emerson Hough
Emilie F. Carlen
Emily Bronte
Emily Dickinson
Enid Bagnold
Enilor Macartney Lane
Erasmus W. Jones
Ernie Howard Pie
Ethel May Dell
Ethel Turner
Ethel Watts Mumford
Eugene Sue
Eugenie Foa
Eugene Wood
Eustace Hale Ball
Evelyn Everett-green
Everard Cotes
F. H. Cheley
F. J. Cross
F. Marion Crawford
Fannie E. Newberry
Federick Austin Ogg
Ferdinand Ossendowski
Fergus Hume
Florence A. Kilpatrick
Fremont B. Deering
Francis Bacon
Francis Darwin
Frances Hodgson Burnett
Frances Parkinson Keyes
Frank Gee Patchin
Frank Harris
Frank Jewett Mather
Frank L. Packard
Frank V. Webster
Frederic Stewart Isham
Frederick Trevor Hill
Frederick Winslow Taylor

Friedrich Kerst
Friedrich Nietzsche
Fyodor Dostoyevsky
G.A. Henty
G.K. Chesterton
Gabrielle E. Jackson
Garrett P. Serviss
Gaston Leroux
George A. Warren
George Ade
Geroge Bernard Shaw
George Cary Eggleston
George Durston
George Ebers
George Eliot
George Gissing
George MacDonald
George Meredith
George Orwell
George Sylvester Viereck
George Tucker
George W. Cable
George Wharton James
Gertrude Atherton
Gordon Casserly
Grace E. King
Grace Gallatin
Grace Greenwood
Grant Allen
Guillermo A. Sherwell
Gulielma Zollinger
Gustav Flaubert
H. A. Cody
H. B. Irving
H.C. Bailey
H. G. Wells
H. H. Munro
H. Irving Hancock
H. R. Naylor
H. Rider Haggard
H. W. C. Davis
Haldeman Julius
Hall Caine
Hamilton Wright Mabie
Hans Christian Andersen
Harold Avery
Harold McGrath
Harriet Beecher Stowe
Harry Castlemon
Harry Coghill
Harry Houidini

Hayden Carruth
Helent Hunt Jackson
Helen Nicolay
Hendrik Conscience
Hendy David Thoreau
Henri Barbusse
Henrik Ibsen
Henry Adams
Henry Ford
Henry Frost
Henry James
Henry Jones Ford
Henry Seton Merriman
Henry W Longfellow
Herbert A. Giles
Herbert Carter
Herbert N. Casson
Herman Hesse
Hildegard G. Frey
Homer
Honore De Balzac
Horace B. Day
Horace Walpole
Horatio Alger Jr.
Howard Pyle
Howard R. Garis
Hugh Lofting
Hugh Walpole
Humphry Ward
Ian Maclaren
Inez Haynes Gillmore
Irving Bacheller
Isabel Cecilia Williams
Isabel Hornibrook
Israel Abrahams
Ivan Turgenev
J.G.Austin
J. Henri Fabre
J. M. Barrie
J. M. Walsh
J. Macdonald Oxley
J. R. Miller
J. S. Fletcher
J. S. Knowles
J. Storer Clouston
J. W. Duffield
Jack London
Jacob Abbott
James Allen
James Andrews
James Baldwin

James Branch Cabell
James DeMille
James Joyce
James Lane Allen
James Lane Allen
James Oliver Curwood
James Oppenheim
James Otis
James R. Driscoll
Jane Abbott
Jane Austen
Jane L. Stewart
Janet Aldridge
Jens Peter Jacobsen
Jerome K. Jerome
Jessie Graham Flower
John Buchan
John Burroughs
John Cournos
John F. Kennedy
John Gay
John Glasworthy
John Habberton
John Joy Bell
John Kendrick Bangs
John Milton
John Philip Sousa
John Taintor Foote
Jonas Lauritz Idemil Lie
Jonathan Swift
Joseph A. Altsheler
Joseph Carey
Joseph Conrad
Joseph E. Badger Jr
Joseph Hergesheimer
Joseph Jacobs
Jules Vernes
Julian Hawthrone
Julie A Lippmann
Justin Huntly McCarthy
Kakuzo Okakura
Karle Wilson Baker
Kate Chopin
Kenneth Grahame
Kenneth McGaffey
Kate Langley Bosher
Kate Langley Bosher
Katherine Cecil Thurston
Katherine Stokes
L. A. Abbot
L. T. Meade

| | | |
|---|---|---|
| L. Frank Baum | Owen Johnson | Stephen Crane |
| Latta Griswold | P.G. Wodehouse | Stewart Edward White |
| Laura Dent Crane | Paul and Mabel Thorne | Stijn Streuvels |
| Laura Lee Hope | Paul G. Tomlinson | Swami Abhedananda |
| Laurence Housman | Paul Severing | Swami Parmananda |
| Lawrence Beasley | Percy Brebner | T. S. Ackland |
| Leo Tolstoy | Percy Keese Fitzhugh | T. S. Arthur |
| Leonid Andreyev | Peter B. Kyne | The Princess Der Ling |
| Lewis Carroll | Plato | Thomas A. Janvier |
| Lewis Sperry Chafer | Quincy Allen | Thomas A Kempis |
| Lilian Bell | R. Derby Holmes | Thomas Anderton |
| Lloyd Osbourne | R. L. Stevenson | Thomas Bailey Aldrich |
| Louis Hughes | R. S. Ball | Thomas Bulfinch |
| Louis Joseph Vance | Rabindranath Tagore | Thomas De Quincey |
| Louis Tracy | Rahul Alvares | Thomas Dixon |
| Louisa May Alcott | Ralph Bonehill | Thomas H. Huxley |
| Lucy Fitch Perkins | Ralph Henry Barbour | Thomas Hardy |
| Lucy Maud Montgomery | Ralph Victor | Thomas More |
| Luther Benson | Ralph Waldo Emmerson | Thornton W. Burgess |
| Lydia Miller Middleton | Rene Descartes | U. S. Grant |
| Lyndon Orr | Ray Cummings | Upton Sinclair |
| M. Corvus | Rex Beach | Valentine Williams |
| M. H. Adams | Rex E. Beach | Various Authors |
| Margaret E. Sangster | Richard Harding Davis | Vaughan Kester |
| Margret Howth | Richard Jefferies | Victor Appleton |
| Margaret Vandercook | Richard Le Gallienne | Victor G. Durham |
| Margaret W. Hungerford | Robert Barr | Victoria Cross |
| Margret Penrose | Robert Frost | Virginia Woolf |
| Maria Edgeworth | Robert Gordon Anderson | Wadsworth Camp |
| Maria Thompson Daviess | Robert L. Drake | Walter Camp |
| Mariano Azuela | Robert Lansing | Walter Scott |
| Marion Polk Angellotti | Robert Lynd | Washington Irving |
| Mark Overton | Robert Michael Ballantyne | Wilbur Lawton |
| Mark Twain | Robert W. Chambers | Wilkie Collins |
| Mary Austin | Rosa Nouchette Carey | Willa Cather |
| Mary Catherine Crowley | Rudyard Kipling | Willard F. Baker |
| Mary Cole | Saint Augustine | William Dean Howells |
| Mary Hastings Bradley | Samuel B. Allison | William le Queux |
| Mary Roberts Rinehart | Samuel Hopkins Adams | W. Makepeace Thackeray |
| Mary Rowlandson | Sarah Bernhardt | William W. Walter |
| M. Wollstonecraft Shelley | Sarah C. Hallowell | William Shakespeare |
| Maud Lindsay | Selma Lagerlof | Winston Churchill |
| Max Beerbohm | Sherwood Anderson | Yei Theodora Ozaki |
| Myra Kelly | Sigmund Freud | Yogi Ramacharaka |
| Nathaniel Hawthrone | Standish O'Grady | Young E. Allison |
| Nicolo Machiavelli | Stanley Weyman | Zane Grey |
| O. F. Walton | Stella Benson | |
| Oscar Wilde | Stella M. Francis | |